WOODWORKING FACTBOOK

Cherry used to carve this vivacious and beautiful horse.

WOODWORKING FACTBOOK

Basic Information on Wood for Wood Carvers, Home Woodshop Craftsmen, Tradesmen, and Instructors.

by

Donald G. Coleman

Chief of the Division of Research

Information and Education of the

Forest Products Laboratory, Madison, Wisconsin

ROBERT SPELLER & SONS
Publishers

NEW YORK 10036

Library of Congress Catalogue Card No. 65-28939
with 73 illustrations
and 5 tables.

First Edition
Photographs are through the courtesy of the Forest Products Laboratory.
PRINTED IN THE UNITED STATES OF AMERICA

To that unheralded corps of technical editors whose sifting and winnowing of vast masses of data make this publication possible.

Preface

Of all the things on earth we need and use, wood is by far the most versatile. It is the outstanding material to delight, console, and enhance the pride of accomplishment of the craftsman. Any count of the uses of wood would reach into thousands — and still be incomplete.

Through countless generations, artisans who built the houses, ships, wagons, printing presses, weapons, and other things learned much about this material. They became familiar with its grain, texture, and hardness; found that some woods carved better, some were stronger, some polished better, and some stayed in place better than did others. With such knowledge handed down from father to son, they devised rules for design with wood and the essentials of carpentry, cabinetmaking, and other crafts.

Inevitably, as knowledge was passed along from master to apprentice, some of the flavor and body of experience that gave it meaning was lost. Learning was by rote, rules supplanted reason why. Thus, today, in many of our modern woodshops, frequented by craftsmen through desire rather than for wages, a need arises for authentic information on wood properties and uses that can be effectively employed without long periods of training or apprenticeship. This publication supplies the need. It is based largely on the work of the engineers, physicists, chemists, and technologists at the U. S. Forest Products Laboratory with whom the author has been associated for more than 30 years and to whom grateful acknowledgement is made hereby.

— Donald G. Coleman

CONTENTS

Introduction

Among all our country's natural resources, none is more remarkable than its wealth of forest materials. In no other nation of the temperate zone is wood available to the people in such abundance and variety, and nowhere else is it used on so large a scale. Not only is wood a main staple of industry and business; it is a medium of expression for ingenuity and the creative impulse, the material of a thousand hobbies. Woodworking may be said to "come natural" to Americans. From the little boy pounding his first nail to the skilled woodworker with fine tools and a modern workshop, all have felt the inward urge to convert a worthy material into forms of utility, interest and beauty.

The constant demand of wood hobbyists, wood sculptures, industrial arts instructors, home craftsmen, and other wood workers for better knowledge of the quality and working properties of all kinds of wood has prompted the preparation of this factbook. It is based largely on experiments and investigations of the U. S. Forest Products Laboratory that the author has been associated with over a period of more than 30 years. Its purpose is to aid woodworkers in the wise selection and use of their material. Technical terms have, as far as possible, been omitted and comparisons of woods confined to simple groupings.

WOODWORKING FACTBOOK

What Wood Is

The uses for which wood is suitable depend upon its properties, that is, upon the way it behaves under various conditions. To understand the properties of wood it is necessary to be familiar with its structure. Wood instead of being a relatively solid material like steel or concrete, is composed of many tubular fiber units cemented together. Seen under a magnifying glass, a piece of wood appears as a honeycomb with openings of various sizes and shapes. The walls together with the cavities of the honeycomb constitute cells, and are formed during the growth of the tree.

Wood Cells

In dry wood the cells are hollow and empty for the most part, although some contain gum or resin of various sorts. Most of the cells in wood are considerably elongated and pointed at the ends, and for that reason are called fibers. The length of wood fibers varies from about one-twenty-fifth inch in hardwoods to from one-eighth to one-third inch in softwoods. The strength of wood, however, does not depend on the length of the fibers, but rather on the thickness and structure of their walls.

In addition to their fibers, hardwoods have cells of relatively large diameters with open ends that comprise the pores, or vessels, through which the sap moves.

In both hardwoods and softwoods strips of cells run at right angles to the fibers, radially in the tree, to conduct sap across the grain. These strips of cells are called rays, wood rays, and medullary rays. In some species of wood the rays are extremely small; in others, such as sycamore and oak, they form the conspicuous flake or silver grain on quarter-sawed surfaces.

Other cells, known as wood parenchyma cells, store food; they occupy a relatively small volume in most woods. In the

1

softwoods there are no special vessels for conducting sap longitudinally in the tree. The wood fibers, which are larger in diameter than the parenchyma cells and technically are called tracheids, serve this function.

The cellular structure is responsible to a large extent for some of the advantages and disadvantages of wood over other structural materials. The cell cavities allow the cell walls to "give" so that nails and screws can readily be driven into lumber, thus affording a comparatively easy means of fastening two pieces together. Because in most commercial woods more than one-half of the volume is occupied by cell cavities, their hardness is such that they can be shaped into various forms with simple tools and with comparatively little labor. Woods with very small cell cavities and thick cell walls, such as lignumvitae, are about as hard as horn and are very difficult to work.

Because of the cavities in the cells, most woods, when dry, are fairly light for a given volume. This is of advantage in the manufacture of furniture and other articles requiring a certain size but not great weight or strength.

The cell cavities act as dead air spaces which retard the transmission of heat and sound. This makes lumber especially adaptable for building purposes, since it tends to keep the heat in during winter and out during summer, and makes the building comparatively soundproof.

Because wood is not a compact homogeneous substance, it absorbs shocks and vibrations to a considerable extent. This makes it particularly suitable for hammer handles, floors, bowling pins, and baseball bats.

The figure in wood, which for some purposes is an important attribute, is due largely to differences in the size and arrangement of its various cells, although irregular deposits of coloring matter also may add to the figure.

Wood may be separated into its component fibers, which, when felted together can be made into paper, wall board, roofing, and the like.

Collectively, the different kinds of cells are spoken of as "elements." A certain size and arrangement of the elements, varying within certain limits, are characteristic of each wood or group of woods, and help in identifying the different kinds and in judging their qualities.

ANNUAL RINGS

Each year a tree adds a layer of wood on the outside of that previously formed, thereby increasing the diameter of the trunk and pushing the bark outward. If growth is interrupted each year, by cold weather or dry seasons, the character of the wood cells at the end of each year's growth and the beginning of the next is sufficiently different to define sharply the annual layers of growth rings (fig. 1). Consequently the age of such a tree may be determined by counting the number of annual rings at the stump.

If the growth of a tree is interrupted during the growing season as a result of drought or defoliation by insects, two or even more separate rings may be formed in the same season. The inner one in such event usually does not have a sharply defined outer boundary; it is called a false ring.

Occasionally, under unfavorable conditions, no growth takes place in parts of a tree trunk, especially in the lower portion. In such a case the annual growth layer is incomplete, portions being entirely missing.

SPRINGWOOD AND SUMMERWOOD

In many species of wood each annual ring is divided more or less distinctly into two layers. The inner one, the springwood, consists of cells having relatively large cavities and frequently thin walls. The outer layer, the summerwood, is composed of smaller cells. The transition from springwood to summerwood may be either abrupt or gradual, depending on the kind of wood and the growing conditions at the time it was formed.

In most trees springwood differs from summerwood in physical properties. It is lighter in weight, softer, and weaker; it shrinks less across and more along the grain; and it is brash in both softwoods and hardwoods.

In some kinds of wood, such as the maples, gums, and yellow-poplar, there is no appreciable difference in the structure and properties of the wood formed early and later in the season.

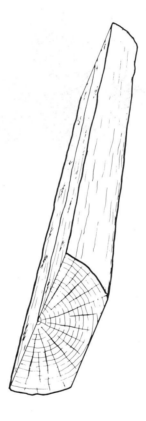

Figure 1.—Cross section of a log showing annual growth rings. Each light ring is springwood. Each dark ring is summerwood. The two together constitute an annual ring.

SAPWOOD AND HEARTWOOD

The sapwood contains living cells and takes an active part in the life processes of the tree. The heartwood consists entirely of inactive tissue and serves primarily to give strength to the tree trunk. As a tree grows in diameter, the inner sapwood changes to heartwood, the change consisting principally in the living cells becoming inactive and small amounts of additional materials, usually colored, being deposited in the cell cavities and the cell walls. In some trees, such as the ashes, hickories, and certain oaks, the pores become plugged to greater or less degree with ingrowths, known as tyloses, before the change from sapwood to heartwood takes place. Sapwood should not be considered as immature or unripe wood but rather as mature living wood, in contrast with the physiologically inactive heartwood.

Sapwood varies greatly in width in different kinds of trees and even in the same species, the width within a species depending on the vigor and the age of the tree. It is rarely more than 1½ inches thick in most of the cedars, Douglas-fir, the spruces, chestnut, and black walnut but frequently is more than 3 inches thick in the maples, hickories, white ash, some of the southern yellow pines, and ponderosa pine.

Although the heartwood is usually darker in color than the sapwood, there is little or no difference between them in color in the spruces (except Sitka spruce), hemlock, the true or balsam firs, Port-Orford-cedar, basswood, cottonwood, and buckeye. Such trees, however, cannot be said to have no heartwood, since other differences in the properties, such as durability and penetrability of liquids, of the inner and outer portions of the tree trunk usually exist.

There is no consistent difference either in the weight when dry or in the strength of sapwood and heartwood. In some trees the sapwood may be heavier and stronger, in others the heartwood, depending on the conditions under which the tree was growing at the time the wood was formed. Wood does not change appreciably in these properties in changing from sapwood to heartwood, except in certain species, such as redwood, western red cedar, and black locust, in which the relatively high percentage of deposited material in the heartwood increases the weight and certain strength properties.

HARDWOODS AND SOFTWOODS

Native trees are divided into two classes — hardwoods, which have broad leaves, and softwoods or conifers, which have leaves like needles or scales.

No definite degree of hardness divides the hardwoods and the softwoods. In fact, many hardwoods are actually softer than the average softwood. Softwoods are frequently called conifers, or coniferous woods, because virtually all the native kinds of softwoods bear cones.

GRAIN AND TEXTURE OF WOOD

The terms "grain" and "texture" are commonly used rather loosely in connection with wood. In fact, they do not have any definite meaning. Grain is often made to refer to the annual rings, as in fine grain and coarse grain, but it is also employed to indicate the direction of the fibers, as in straight grain, spiral grain, and curly grain. Painters refer to woods as open-grained and close-grained, meaning thereby the relative size of the pores, which determines whether the piece needs a filler. Texture is often used synonymously with grain, but usually it refers to the finer structure of the wood rather than to the annual rings. When the words "grain" or "texture" are used in connection with wood, the meaning intended should be made perfectly clear.

PLAIN-SAWED AND QUARTER-SAWED LUMBER

Lumber can be cut from a log in two distinct ways, namely, tangent to the annual rings, producing what is known as "plain-sawed" lumber in hardwoods and "flat-grain" or "slash-grain" lumber in softwoods, and parallel to the radiuses, or rays, producing what is known as "quarter-sawed" lumber in hardwoods and "edge-grain" or "vertical-grain" lumber in softwoods (fig. 2). Usually so-called quarter-sawed or edge-grain lumber is not cut strictly parallel with the rays; and often in plain-sawed boards the surfaces next to the edges are far from being tangent to the rings. It is commercial practice to call material with rings from 45° to 90° with the surface quarter-sawed, while material with rings from 0° to 45° with the surface is

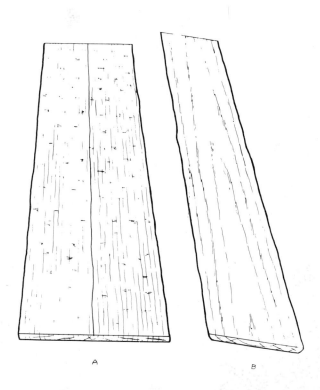

Figure 2. — *Quarter-sawed* (A) *and plain-sawed* (B) *boards cut from log.*

called plain-sawed. Hardwood lumber in which the annual rings make angles of 30° to 60° with the faces is sometimes called "bastard sawn."

Following are some of the advantages of plain-sawed, or flat-grain lumber:

(1) It is cheaper, as a rule, because it requires less time and involves less waste in cutting.

(2) The figure resulting from the annual rings and also some other types of figure are brought out most conspicuously.

(3) Round or oval knots which may occur in plain-sawed boards affect the surface appearance less than spike knots which may occur in quarter-sawed boards. Also a board with a round or oval knot is weakened less by the knot than a board with a spike knot. However, a greater percentage of the boards from a log sawed to produce the maximum amount of plain-sawed lumber will contain knots than do boards from a log sawed to produce the maximum amount of quarter-sawed material.

(4) Shakes and pitch pockets when present extend through fewer boards.

(5) It does not collapse so easily in drying.

Following are the principal advantages of quarter-sawed or edge-grain lumber:

(1) It shrinks and swells less in width.

(2) It twists and cups less.

(3) It does not surface check or split so badly in seasoning and in use.

(4) Raised grain caused by the annual rings does not become so pronounced.

(5) It wears more evenly.

(6) Types of figure coming from pronounced rays, interlocked grain, and wavy grain are brought out most conspicuously.

(7) It does not allow liquids to pass into or through it so readily.

(8) It holds paint better in some species.

(9) The width of the sapwood appearing in a board is limited according to the width of the sapwood in the log.

DECORATIVE FEATURES OF COMMON WOODS

The decorative value of wood depends upon its color, figure, luster, and the way in which it takes fillers, stain, fumes, and transparent finishes.

Because of the combinations of color and the number of shades found in wood, it is impossible to give detailed descriptions of the colors of the various kinds. The sapwood of all species, however, is light in color and in some species it is practically white. The white sapwood of certain species, such as maple, makes it preferable to the heartwood for specific uses. In some species, such as hemlock, the true firs, basswood, cottonwood, and beech, there is little difference in color between sapwood and heartwood, but in most species the heartwood is darker and fairly uniform in color. Table 1 describes in a general way the color of the heartwood of the more common kinds of woods.

Some types of figure are more pronounced in plain-sawed lumber and others in quarter-sawed (table 1). Often lumber is neither strictly plain-sawed or strictly quarter-sawed but rather is intermediate, thereby losing some of its decorative effect.

In plain-sawed boards and rotary-cut veneer the annual growth rings frequently form ellipses and parabolas that make striking figures, especially when the rings are irregular in width and outline on the cut surface (fig. 3). On quarter-sawed surfaces these rings form stripes, which are not especially ornamental unless they are irregular in width and direction (fig. 4). The relatively large rays, often referred to as flakes, form a conspicuous figure in quarter-sawed oak and sycamore. With interlocked grain, which slopes in alternate directions in successive layers from the center of the tree outward, quarter-sawed surfaces show a ribbon effect, either because of the difference in reflection of light from successive layers when the wood has a natural luster or because cross grain of varying degree absorbs stains unevenly. Much of this type of figure is lost in plain-sawed lumber.

In open-grained hardwoods, the appearance of both plain-sawed and quarter-sawed lumber can be varied greatly by the use of fillers of different colors. In softwoods the annual growth layers can be made to stand out more by applying a stain.

Table 1.—*Color and figure of common kinds of wood*

HARDWOODS

Species	Color of heartwood[1]	Type of figure in —	
		Plainsawed lumber or rotary-cut veneer	Quartersawed lumber or quarter-sliced veneer
Alder, red......................	Pale pinkish brown....	Faint growth ring....	Scattered large flakes, sometimes entirely absent.
Ash:			
Black............................	Moderately dark grayish brown.	Conspicuous growth ring; occasional burl.	Distinct, not conspicuous growth-ring stripe; occasional burl.
Oregon..........................	Grayish brown, sometimes with reddish tinge.	........do............................	Do.
White............................	........do............................	........do............................	Do.
Aspen................................	Light brown................	Faint growth ring......	None.
Basswood..........................	Creamy white to creamy brown, sometimes reddish.	........do............................	Do.
Beech, American............	White with reddish tinge, to reddish brown.	........do............................	Numerous small flakes up to ⅛ inch in height.
Birch:			
Paper............................	Light brown................	........do............................	None.
Sweet............................	Dark reddish brown....	Distinct, not conspicuous growth ring; occasionally wavy.	Occasionally wavy.
Yellow..........	Reddish brown............		Do.
Buttternut........................	Light chestnut brown with occasional reddish tinge or streaks.	Faint growth ring......	None.
Cherry, black..................	Light to dark reddish brown.	Faint growth ring; occasional burl.	Occasional burl.
Chestnut, American......	Grayish brown............	Conspicuous growth ring.	Distinct, not conspicuous growth-ring stripe.
Cottonwood......................	Grayish white to light grayish brown.	Faint growth ring......	None.
Elm:			
American and rock..	Light grayish brown, usually with reddish tinge.	Distinct, not conspicuous, with fine wavy pattern within each growth ring.	Faint growth-ring stripe.
Slippery........................	Dark brown with shades of red.	Conspicuous growth ring, with fine pattern within each growth ring.	Distinct, not conspicuous growth-ring stripe.
Hackberry........................	Light yellowish or greenish gray.	Conspicuous growth ring.	Distinct, not conspicuous growth-ring stripe.
Hickory............................	Reddish brown............	Distinct, not conspicuous growth ring.	Faint growth-ring stripe.

See footnotes at end of table.

TABLE 1.—*Color and figure of common kinds of wood*—Continued

HARDWOODS

Species	Color of heartwood[1]	Type of figure in —	
		Plainsawed lumber or rotary-cut veneer	Quartersawed lumber or quarter-sliced veneer
Honeylocust....................	Cherry red........	Conspicuous growth ring.	Distinct, not conspicuous growth-ring stripe.
Locust, black..................	Golden brown, sometimes with tinge of green.	Conspicuous growth rings.	Do.
Magnolia..........................	Light to dark yellowish brown with greenish or purplish tinge.	Faint growth ring......	None.
Maple: Black, bigleaf, silver, and sugar.	Light reddish brown	Faint growth ring, occasionally birdseye, curly, and wavy.	Occasionally curly and wavy.
Oak: All species of red oak group.	Grayish brown, usually with fleshy tinge.	Conspicuous growth ring.	Pronounced flake; distinct, not conspicuous growth-ring stripe.
All species of white oak group.	Grayish brown, rarely with fleshy tinge.	........do...........................	Do.
Sugarberry.......................	Light yellowish or greenish gray.	........do...........................	Distinct, not conspicuous growth-ring stripe.
Sweetgum......	Reddish brown............	Faint growth ring, occasionally irregular darker streaks in "figured" gum.	Distinct, not pronounced ribbon; occasionally irregular darker streaks in "figured" gum.
Sycamore..........................	Flesh brown..............	Faint growth ring......	Numerous pronounced flakes up to ¼ inch in height.
Tupelo: Black and water..........................	Pale to moderately dark brownish gray.	........do...........................	Distinct, not pronounced ribbon.
Walnut, black.................	Chocolate brown occasionally with darker, sometimes purplish streaks.	Distinct, not conspicuous growth ring; occasionally wavy, curly, burl, and other types.	Distinct, not conspicuous growth-ring stripe. occasionally wavy, curly, burl, crotch, and other types.
Yellow-poplar.................	Light to dark yellowish brown with greenish or purplish tinge.	Faint growth ring......	None.

SOFTWOODS

Baldcypress.....................	Light yellowish brown to reddish brown.	Conspicuous irregular growth ring.	Distinct, not conspicuous growth-ring stripe.
Cedar: Alaska-	Yellow.........................	Faint growth ring......	None.
Atlantic white-	Light brown with reddish tinge.	Distinct, not conspicuous growth ring.	Do.

See footnotes at end of table.

TABLE 1.—*Color and figure of common kinds of wood*—Continued

SOFTWOODS

Species	Color of heartwood[1]	Type of figure in —	
		Plainsawed lumber or rotary-cut veneer	Quartersawed lumber or quarter-sliced veneer
Cedar—Continued			
Eastern redcedar	Brick red to deep reddish brown.	Occasionally streaks of white sapwood alternating with heartwood.	Occasionally streaks of white sapwood alternating with heartwood.
Incense-	Reddish brown	Faint growth ring	Faint growth-ring stripe.
Northern white-	Light to dark brown	........do	Do.
Port-Orford-	Light yellow to pale brown.	........do	None.
Western redcedar	Reddish brown	Distinct, not conspicuous growth ring.	Faint growth-ring stripe.
Douglas-fir	Orange red to red; sometimes yellow.	Conspicuous growth ring.	Distinct, not conspicuous growth-ring stripe.
Fir:			
Balsam	Nearly white	Distinct, not conspicuous growth ring.	Faint growth-ring stripe.
White	Nearly white to pale reddish brown.	Conspicuous growth ring.	Distinct, not conspicuous growth-ring stripe.
Hemlock:			
Eastern	Light reddish brown	Distinct, not conspicuous growth ring.	Faint growth-ring stripe.
Western	........do	........do	Do.
Larch, western	Russet to reddish brown.	Conspicuous growth ring.	Distinct, not conspicuous growth-ring stripe.
Pine:			
Eastern white	Cream to light reddish brown.	Faint growth ring	None.
Lodgepole	Light reddish brown	Distinct, not conspicuous growth ring; faint "pocked" appearance.	Do.
Ponderosa	Orange to reddish brown.	Distinct, not conspicuous growth ring.	Faint growth-ring stripe.
Red	........do	........do	Do.
Southern yellow[1]	........do	Conspicuous growth ring.	Distinct, not conspicuous growth-ring stripe.
Sugar	Light creamy brown	Faint growth ring	None.
Western white	Cream to light reddish brown.	........do	Do.
Redwood	Cherry to deep reddish brown.	Distinct, not conspicuous growth ring; occasionally wavy and burl.	Faint growth-ring stripe; occasionally wavy and burl.
Spruce:			
Black, Engelmann, red, white.	Nearly white	Faint growth ring	None.
Sitka	Light reddish brown	Distinct, not conspicuous growth ring.	Faint growth-ring stripe.
Tamarack	Russet brown	Conspicuous growth ring.	Distinct, not conspicuous growth-ring stripe.

[1] The sapwood of all species is light in color or virtually white unless discolored by fungus or chemical stains.
[2] Includes longleaf, loblolly, shortleaf, and slash pine.

Figure 3. — A. Growth-ring figure in plain-sawed oak. B. Growth-ring figure in rotary-cut oak veneer.

Figure 4.— A. Stripe figure in tanguile. B. Stripe figure in black walnut.

STUMP OR BUTT WOOD

At the junction of the larger roots with the stem of a tree and to a less extent where the branches join the stem, the fibers are considerably distorted, producing various kinds of cross figure, particularly mottle and curly grain. Veneers cut from such portions of the tree are highly figured and command a high price. Black walnut stumps find a ready market at veneer plants for this reason. Such veneers are usually matched so as to produce a panel with a symmetrical pattern.

CROTCH

At forks in the tree trunk and where large branches join the trunk, the fibers run in different directions in closely adjoining portions, often giving lumber cut from such parts of a tree a pattern resembling a cluster of plumes (fig. 5, *A*). This is called "crotch figure", or, more often, "crotch mahogany", "crotch walnut", etc., according to the kind of wood.

BLISTER

Blister consists of seeming knoll-like elevations in the wood, as shown in figure 5, *B*. It is due to an uneven contour of the annual rings, and not to blisters or pockets in the wood as the name might indicate. It occurs in various species and is pronounced only in plain-sawed lumber or rotary-cut veneer.

BURLS

Burls are large wart-like excrescences on tree trunks. They contain the dark piths of a large number of buds. The formation of these buds, which rarely develop, apparently is due to some injury sustained by the tree. Throughout the burl the fibers are very irregularly contorted so that the grain cannot be said to run in any particular direction. Burls may occur on almost any species, but walnut, ash, cherry, and redwood burls are among the most highly prized in furniture woods. Figure 6, *A*, shows burl in cherry.

Figure 5.— A. Crotch figure in mahogany. B. Blister figure in mahogany.

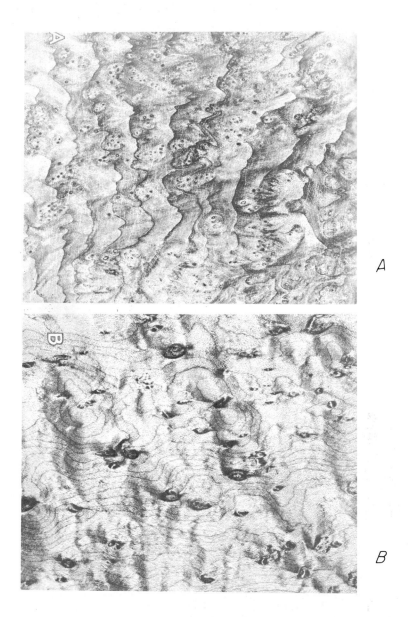

Figure 6.—A. Cherry burl. B. Bird's-eye maple.

Bird's-eye

Bird's-eye is due to local sharp depressions in the annual rings, accompanied by considerable fiber distortion. Once the depressions are formed, succeeding growth rings follow the same contour for many years. In plain-sawed lumber and rotary veneer the depressions are cut through crosswise and show a series of circlets, portions of annual rings, suggesting, rather remotely, a bird's eye (fig. 5, B). Among native commercial woods typical bird's-eye figure is confined almost exclusively to maple, and it occurs in only a small percentage of maple trees. It differs from burl in that burl is due to conical elevations each containing a dark speck, the pith of a bud. Burl also shows greater distortion of fibers throughout. It is not clear what causes the irregularities which give rise to bird's-eye figure.

Knots, pin wormholes, bird pecks, mineral streaks, swirls, and bark are decorative in some species when the wood is carefully selected for a particular architectural treatment.

Weathering of Wood

Boards exposed to the weather without a protective coating rapidly become weathered. Weathering may involve change in color, roughening and checking of the surface, and, if one side of the board only is fully exposed, cupping and tearing loose from fastenings, but it does not include decay. With all species, edge-grain boards check less conspicuously and cup less than flat-grain boards of the same species. Twisting, another although less common effect of weathering, is caused primarily by uneven shrinkage resulting from spiral and interlocked grain; it is more pronounced in plain-sawed than in quarter-sawed boards. Weathering, as a rule, changes all woods to a gray color, darker in some woods than in others, and attractive when accompanied by a silvery sheen, as it often is. (See pp. 19 and 20.)

Identification of Wood

The color, odor, or general appearance is usually sufficiently distinctive to identify a sample of wood. Characteristics that are apparent to the naked eye and that distinguish our native woods from each other are described here for each of 32 species (plates I - XVI). Because color is an important characteristic in identifying many woods, special attention has been paid to describing the natural color of a freshly cut surface of the wood.

Descriptions of species are accompanied by full-color illustrations showing grain pattern and other characteristics. Beginning at the top of the illustration, end-grained, edge-grained

Woods that weather with —

Light-gray color and silvery sheen
- Baldcypress
- Cedar, Alaska
- Cedar, Port-Orford

Light-gray color and moderate sheen
- Aspen
- Basswood
- Birch
- Cottonwood
- Hemlock, eastern
- Hemlock, western
- Hickory
- Maple
- Pine, eastern white
- Pine, ponderosa
- Pine, sugar
- Pine, western white
- Spruce, eastern
- Spruce, Sitka
- Sweetgum
- Yellow-poplar

Dark-gray color and little or no sheen
- Ash
- Cedar, westernred
- Chestnut
- Douglas-fir
- Fir, commercial white
- Larch, western
- Oak, red
- Oak, white
- Pine, southern yellow
- Redwood
- Walnut, black

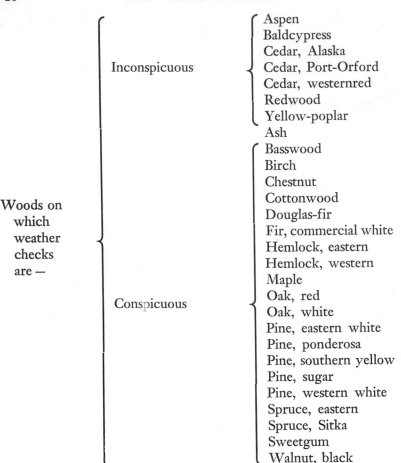

Woods on which weather checks are —

Inconspicuous
- Aspen
- Baldcypress
- Cedar, Alaska
- Cedar, Port-Orford
- Cedar, westernred
- Redwood
- Yellow-poplar

Conspicuous
- Ash
- Basswood
- Birch
- Chestnut
- Cottonwood
- Douglas-fir
- Fir, commercial white
- Hemlock, eastern
- Hemlock, western
- Maple
- Oak, red
- Oak, white
- Pine, eastern white
- Pine, ponderosa
- Pine, southern yellow
- Pine, sugar
- Pine, western white
- Spruce, eastern
- Spruce, Sitka
- Sweetgum
- Walnut, black

(quarter sawed), and flat-grained (plain sawed) surfaces are all displayed. This is done because certain identifying characteristics show up best on each surface. The terms "edge-grained" and "flat-grained" are used in reference to softwood lumber, while quarter sawed and plain sawed refer to hardwood lumber.

The manner in which it is sawed from the log will, of course, determine whether a piece of wood shows flat-grained or edge-grained patterns of annual growth rings on its wide surfaces. Lumber is manufactured in both forms.

Each color plate presents two species. Where possible,

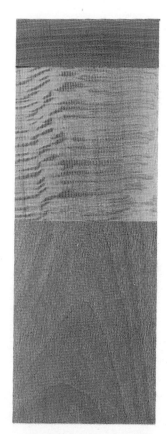

AMERICAN BEECH   AMERICAN SYCAMORE

ROCK ELM   AMERICAN ELM

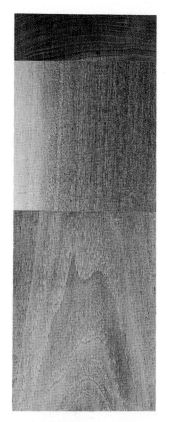

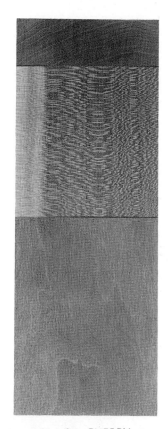

BLACK WALNUT   BLACK CHERRY

TRUE HICKORY   WHITE ASH

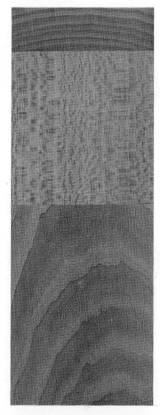

QUAKING ASPEN   AMERICAN BASSWOOD

SWEETGUM   BLACK TUPELO

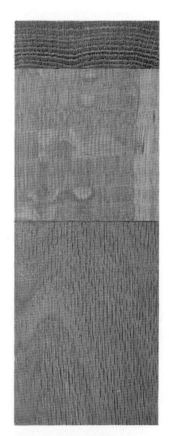

WHITE OAK   RED OAK

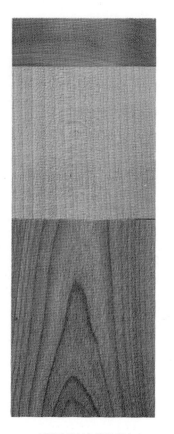

YELLOW BIRCH   SUGAR MAPLE

YELLOW - POPLAR   EASTERN COTTONWOOD

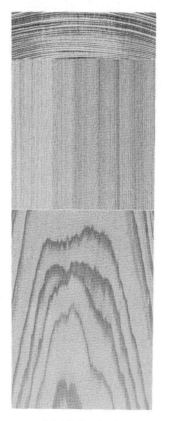 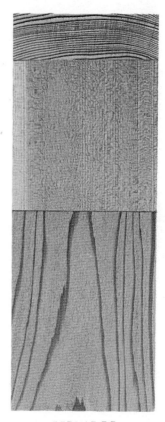

BALDCYPRESS   REDWOOD

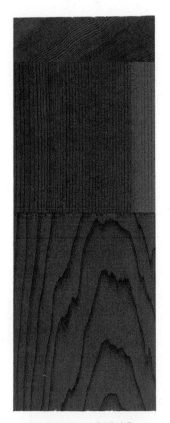

INCENSE - CEDAR   WESTERN REDCEDAR

SHORTLEAF PINE   PONDEROSA PINE

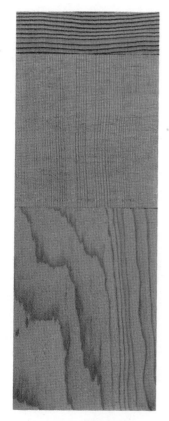

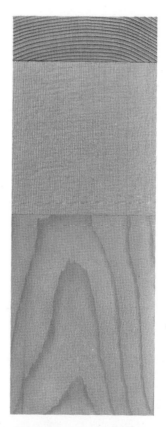

SITKA SPRUCE   ENGELMANN SPRUCE

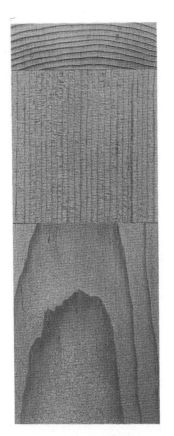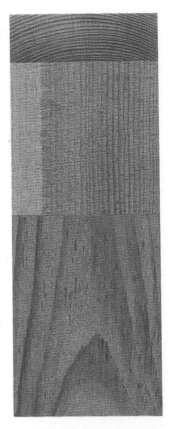

SUGAR PINE　　　　WESTERN WHITE PINE

WESTERN LARCH   DOUGLAS-FIR

 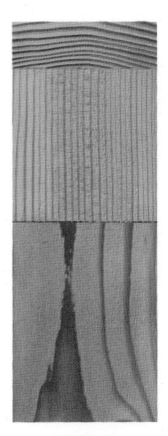

WESTERN HEMLOCK   WHITE FIR

closely similar species are shown together on one plate, so that distinguishing characteristics can be more conveniently examined. In other cases, species are paired on one plate because they are often marketed in mixture or used interchangeably.

Certain species are not distinguishable from close relatives by the wood alone, even under the microscope. Thus, for example, the wood of many different species of red oak is identical in structure and appearance even though the trees from which it comes may differ markedly in leaf, bark, and fruit. From the wood user's standpoint, however, botanical differences in trees usually do not matter so long as their wood is consistent in properties and appearance. Where appropriate in the descriptions, differences are mentioned that distinguish a species from closely similar ones not shown.

Obviously, many other species could have been included with the 18 hardwoods and 14 softwoods described in this publication. Those chosen are the species most commonly found in retail lumber markets.

AMERICAN BEECH

Description. — Heartwood is white with a reddish tinge to reddish brown. Pores are not visible but wood rays can be seen on all surfaces. On the end grain, the rays appear to be irregularly spaced, while on quartersawed surfaces they appear to be of different heights along the grain. On the plainsawed surfaces, the rays also appear to be of different height, but they look much narrower in this view. Beech is readily distinguishable from other native species by its weight, conspicuous rays, and tiny pores.

AMERICAN SYCAMORE

Description. — Heartwood is reddish brown or flesh brown in color. Pores are very small and not visible to the unaided eye. Rays are visible on all surfaces. They appear uniformly spaced on the end grain and of uniform height on quartersawed surfaces. Plainsawed surfaces show rays that appear more numerous and more closely spaced than in beech.

ROCK ELM

Description. — Heartwood is brown to dark brown, sometimes with shades of red. Summerwood pores are arranged in concentric wavy lines that appear lighter than the background wood. The springwood pores in rock elm are visible only upon magnification.

AMERICAN ELM

Description. — Heartwood is brown to dark brown, sometimes containing shades of red. Although the summerwood pores are not visible as individuals, they are arranged in concentric wavy lines within the boundaries of the growth rings. The wavy lines appear lighter than the background wood. American elm shows a springwood pore zone with a single row of large and easily visible pores.

BLACK CHERRY

Description. — Has light to dark reddish brown heartwood. Individual pores are not visible to the naked eye. On end-grain surfaces, the pores may appear to form lines that parallel the growth rings, while on plainsawed surfaces, they may follow the outline of the growth-ring boundary.

The wood rays of cherry are barely visible on end-grain surfaces and tend to produce a distinctive flake pattern on true quartersawed surfaces. They are higher along the grain than those of walnut and hence show more prominently on quartersawed surfaces.

BLACK WALNUT

Description. — Heartwood is chocolate brown and occasionally has darker, sometimes purplish, streaks. Unless bleached or otherwise modified, black walnut is not easily confused with any other native species. Pores are barely visible on the end grain but are quite easily seen as darker streaks or grooves on longitudinal surfaces. Arrangement of pores is similar to that in the hickories and persimmon, but the pores are smaller in size.

TRUE HICKORY

Description. — Heartwood is brown to reddish brown. Pores are visible, but the zone of large pores is not sharply outlined as in oak and ash. Pores grade in size from one side of the annual ring to the other. Wood rays are very small and seen without magnification only on quartersawed surfaces.

Tyloses frequently plug the pores, making their outlines indistinct. Under magnification, the end grain shows numerous white lines paralleling the growth ring.

WHITE ASH

Description. — Heartwood is brown to dark brown, sometimes with a reddish tint. The zone of large pores is usually sharply defined. The small wood rays are generally visible only on quartersawed surfaces. The zone of large pores is more distinctive in ash than in hickory. Also, the summerwood zone in ash shows white dots or lines that are visible to the unaided eye, but in hickory these dots or lines are visible only upon magnification.

QUAKING ASPEN

Description. — Heartwood is white to very light brown, with occasional brown streaks associated with defects. Pores are very small and generally not visible to the unaided eye. Growth rings are usually faint. Wood rays are small, uniform in height along the grain, and visible only on quartersawed surfaces. Aspen is similar to cottonwood, but cottonwood tends to have barely visible pores. The growth rings in aspen are generally narrower than those in cottonwood.

BASSWOOD

Description. — Heartwood is creamy white to creamy brown to sometimes reddish. Pores are very small, as in aspen, and growth rings on plainsawed surfaces are generally faint. Wood rays are broader and higher than in aspen, and the two species can be readily distinguished by comparing their quartersawed faces. While the rays of aspen are low and uniform in height, some of those in basswood are distinctly higher than others and frequently darker than the background wood.

SWEETGUM

Description. — Heartwood is reddish brown and occasionally variegated with streaks of darker color. Pores are so small that they are not visible except upon magnification. Growth rings are usually indistinct or inconspicuous. Rays are visible on quartersawed faces.

BLACK TUPELO

Description. — Heartwood is pale to moderately dark

brownish gray or dirty gray. Pores are very small, as in sweet-gum. Growth rings are generally inconspicuous to moderately distinct. Rays are visible on quartersawed surfaces, but show up less prominently against the background color of the wood than the rays in sweetgum.

WHITE OAK

Description. — Heartwood is grayish brown. The outlines of the larger pores are indistinct except in chestnut oak, which has open pores with distinct outlines. On smooth-cut, end-grain surfaces, the summerwood pores are not distinct as individuals. Wood rays are generally higher than in red oak, the larger ones ranging from 1/2 to 5 inches in height along the grain. As in red oak, rays appear lighter in color than the background wood on end-grain surfaces and darker than the background wood on sidegrain surfaces.

RED OAK

Description. — Heartwood is grayish brown with a more or less distinctive reddish tint. Pores are commonly open, and the outlines of the larger pores are distinct. On smoothly cut end-grain surfaces, the summerwood pores can be seen as individuals and readily counted when examined with a hand lens. Wood rays are commonly 1/4 to 1 inch high along the grain. On end-grain surfaces, rays appear as lines crossing the growth rings.

YELLOW BIRCH

Description. — Yellow birch heartwood is light reddish brown. Pores are very small, sometimes just barely visible on smoothly cut end-grain surfaces, and are uniformly distributed through the annual ring cross section. Pore lines are visible on longitudinal surfaces as very fine grooves that may even be seen through natural finishes. Wood rays may be seen only on quartersawed surfaces, where they appear to be of one size and of uniform height along the grain. Growth rings are moderately distinct on plainsawed surfaces.

SUGAR MAPLE

Description. — Heartwood is light reddish brown and sometimes shows greenish-black streaks near injuries. Pores are extremely small and not visible on any surface. Wood rays may be seen on the end grain and especially on quartersawed faces, where the higher rays are distinctive because of their color and size and smaller rays appear as fine lines between them. The wood rays may also be seen on plainsawed surfaces as very small darker colored flecks that are parallel to the grain of the wood.

YELLOW-POPLAR

Description. — Heartwood is brownish yellow, usually with a definite greenish tinge. The wood rays, as seen on a smoothly cut end-grain surface, are somewhat more prominent than in cucumbertree. Positive identification of yellow-poplar and cucumbertree is best accomplished microscopically, but it is possible to separate them on the basis of gross features when both woods are at hand.

COTTONWOOD

Description. — Heartwood of all three cottonwood species is grayish white to light grayish brown with occasional streaks of light brown. The annual rings are rather wide. Pores are barely visible on smooth cut, end-grain surfaces. Aside from the color of the heartwood, cottonwood is extremely similar to black willow. Separation of the two species is based mainly on heartwood color, which is light brown or reddish brown in willow, or on microscopic examination if only sapwood material is available.

BALDCYPRESS

Description. — Heartwood varies in color from pale brown to blackish brown and sometimes has a reddish tinge. The wood is without resin canals, and transition from springwood to summerwood is abrupt, as in redwood. Heartwood of darker specimens generally has a more or less rancid odor and longitudinal surfaces feel distinctly greasy or waxy.

REDWOOD

Description. — Heartwood is usually a uniform deep reddish brown. The wood is without resin canals and has no distinctive odor, taste, or feel. Western redcedar may approach redwood in color, but the distinctive odor of western redcedar separates the two woods immediately.

INCENSE-CEDAR

Description.— Heartwood is reddish brown to dull brown, with an occasional tinge of lavender and has a cedarlike odor and acrid taste. Transition from springwood to summerwood is more or less abrupt and makes the growth rings prominent on flat-grained surfaces. It is easier to produce a smooth cut on the end grain of incense-cedar than on western redcedar. Although incense-cedar and western redcedar cannot always be separated with certainty on the basis of gross features, they can be readily distinguished under the microscope.

WESTERN REDCEDAR

Description. — Heartwood is reddish or pinkish brown to dull brown. It has a characteristic cedarlike odor, but shavings placed on the tongue do not give quite the sensation that incense-cedar shavings do. Transition from springwood to summerwood is the same as in incense-cedar. The wood is sometimes confused with redwood, but the cedarlike odor of western redcedar separates the two species immediately.

SHORTLEAF PINE

Description. — Heartwood ranges from shades of yellow and orange to reddish brown or light brown. Transition from springwood to summerwood is abrupt, with the annual rings prominent on all surfaces. Resin canals are large and abundant and are easily found in all annual rings. Summerwood bands are generally wider than those of ponderosa pine. In appearance, the wood of shortleaf pine closely resembles that of longleaf, loblolly, and slash, the other principal southern pines.

PONDEROSA PINE

Description. — Heartwood is yellowish to light reddish or orange brown. Transition from springwood to summerwood is abrupt. Growth rings are generally most prominent on the flat-grained surfaces, which also frequently exhibit a dimpled appearance. The resin canals of ponderosa pine are abundant and easily found in all annual rings.

SITKA SPRUCE

Description. — Heartwood is light pinkish yellow to pale brown. Transition from springwood to summerwood is gradual, making the annual rings appear rather inconspicuous on flat-grained surfaces. Resin canals are usually more prominent than in the other spruces. On end-grain surfaces, the canals appear as small dots or very short lines that run parallel to the growth ring. Flat-grained surfaces are lustrous and frequently exhibit dimpling. The pinkish color of the heartwood distinguishes this species from all other spruces.

ENGELMANN SPRUCE

Description. — Heartwood is not distinct from sapwood and ranges from nearly white to pale yellowish brown. Transition from springwood to summerwood is somewhat more abrupt than in the other spruces. Resin canals are present, but are frequently difficult to find. They appear on very smoothly cut, end-grain sections as small white dots and on longitudinal surfaces as short, light-brown streaks or very fine grooves. The wood of all the spruces, with the exception of Sitka, is very similar in its gross and microscopic features and therefore almost impossible to tell apart.

SUGAR PINE

Description. — Heartwood is light brown to pale reddish brown. Resin canals are abundant and commonly stain the surface of the wood with resin. Transition from springwood to summerwood is gradual; making the growth rings appear less prominent on flat-grained surfaces.

WESTERN WHITE PINE

Description. — Heartwood is cream colored to light brown or reddish brown. Resin canals are abundant and transition from springwood to summerwood is like that in sugar pine. Separation of western white pine and sugar pine is generally accomplished on the basis of the resin canals, which are larger in sugar pine than in the other white pines. Microscopic characteristics, however, offer a more reliable means of differentiation than gross features.

WESTERN LARCH

Description. — Heartwood is russet brown and the color is best seen in summerwood bands on flat-grained surfaces. Resin canals are present, but are very small and difficult to find unless the resin has stained the wood surfaces or the exudation actually appears as very small droplets. Transition from spring-wood to summerwood is abrupt and there is little difference in color between the two zones. The heartwood lacks a distinctive odor.

DOUGLAS-FIR

Description. — Heartwood is orange red to red or some-times yellowish. Resin canals, which are seen as brownish streaks in the summerwood, appear to be more abundant and more readily detectable than in western larch. Transition from spring-wood to summerwood is similar to that in western larch. The heartwood of Douglas-fir may be confused with that of the southern yellow pines, but resin canals are larger and much more abundant in southern pines. Most Douglas-fir has a distinctive odor.

WESTERN HEMLOCK

Description. — Heartwood of western hemlock is light reddish brown and frequently has a purplish cast, especially in the summerwood bands. Transition from springwood to sum-merwood is gradual and on end-grain surfaces there is little color contrast between the two zones. The wood lacks normal resin canals. A smooth cut is difficult to make on the end grain of eastern hemlock, even with a very sharp knife, while western hemlock cuts very easily and produces smooth surfaces.

WHITE FIR

Description. — Heartwood is nearly white to pale reddish brown and the wood lacks normal resin canals. Transition from springwood, like that in eastern hemlock, is more abrupt than in western hemlock. Also, color of springwood and summer-wood on end-grain surfaces is more contrasting than in western hemlock. The balsam fir of the east is more uniformly white in color, with less contrasting rings than the western firs.

CHARACTERISTICS OF SOME IMPORTED WOODS

The gross features, shrinkage, mechanical properties and use of 15 botanical species imported into the United States are described. These are listed alphabetically under their common or trade names. Owing to the fact that many of these exotic species have numerous local or trade names, the botanical names are also given to aid in their exact identification.

BALSA (*Ochroma Lagopus* Sw.)

Balsa is widely distributed throughout tropical America from southern Mexico to southern Brazil and Bolivia, but Ecuador has been the principal area of growth since the wood gained commercial importance.

Balsa possesses several characteristics that make possible a wide variety of uses. It is the lightest and softest of all woods on the market. The lumber when dry weighs on the average of about 11 pounds per cubic foot and often as little as 6 pounds. Because of its light weight and exceedingly porous composition, balsa is highly efficient in uses where buoyancy, insulation against heat and cold, or absorption of sound and vibration are important considerations.

The wood is readily recognized by its light weight, white to very pale gray color, and its unique "velvety" feel.

The principal uses of balsa are in life-saving equipment, floats, rafts, core stock, insulation, cushioning, sound modifiers, models, and novelties. Balsa is imported at the rate of 12 to 15 million board feet annually and is imported in larger volume than most of the foreign woods entering the United States.

BOXWOOD, MARACAIBO (*Gossypiospermum Praecos* [Gris.] P. Wilson)

Maracaibo boxwood, Venezuelan boxwood, or West Indian boxwood, is a small - to medium-sized tree native to Dominican Republic, Cuba, the Maracaibo Lake region of Venezuela, and eastern Colombia. The timber found in the United States markets is almost exclusively of Venezuelan origin with occasional small lots from Cuba.

The wood is lemon yellow to nearly white in color, with a very fine and uniform texture. Its grain is generally straight, it is easy to carve and turn, and finishes very smoothly with a high natural polish. The wood is hard and heavy, weighing between 50 to 56 pounds per cubic foot air dry.

This species is by far the most important boxwood commercially, and it has very largely replaced Turkish boxwood

(*Buxus sempervirens* L.) for all purposes except the finest engraving blocks. The principal use of the wood is for the manufacture of precision rules. Other uses include engravers' blocks, carving, and turning.

CATIVO (*Prioria Copaifera* Gris.)

Cativo is one of the few tropical American species that occur in abundance and often in nearly pure stands. Commercial stands are found in Nicaragua, Costa Rica, Panama, and Colombia. The sapwood is usually thick, and in trees up to 30 inches in diameter the heartwood may be only 7 inches in diameter. The sapwood that is utilized commercially may be a very pale-pinkish color or may be distinctly reddish. The grain is straight and the texture of the wood is uniform, comparable to that of mahogany. Figure on flat-sawn surfaces is rather subdued and results from the exposure of the narrow bands of parenchyma tissue. Odor and taste are not distinctive, and the luster is low.

The wood can be seasoned rapidly and easily with very little degrade. The dimensional stability of the wood is very good; it is practically equal to that of mahogany. Cativo is classed as a nondurable wood with respect to decay and insects. Cativo may contain appreciable quantities of gum, which may interfere with finishes. In wood that has been properly seasoned, however, the gum presents no difficulties.

Considerable quantities are used for interior trim, and resin-stabilized veneer has become an important pattern material, particularly in the automotive industry. Cativo is widely used for furniture and cabinet parts, lumber core for plywood, picture frames, edge banding for doors, and bases for piano keyboards.

EBONY (*Diospyros* spp.)

The true ebony of the trade is the product of a number of species, which are widely distributed throughout the tropics of the world. Many of these have overlapping ranges and are very similar botanically. In a few instances, the botanical source of the commercial ebonies is known with certainty and the wood can be definitely stated to be the product of a given species. The identity of the great majority, however, is still in doubt, and it is the practice to apply adjective modifications that indicate the geographical source of the timber, such as Indian ebony, Ceylon ebony, and Gabon ebony. The ebonies also are classified into two distinct color groups: Black ebony includes woods of a uniform black color; whereas streaked ebony woods, as the term implies, are striated with darker and lighter zones.

The heartwood is extremely hard, heavy, and difficult to work. The black ebonies weigh about 73 pounds per cubic foot seasoned, while the streaked ebonies weight about 63 pounds per cubic foot in the seasoned condition.

GREENHEART (*Ocotea Rodiaei* [Schomb.] Mez.)

Greenheart is essentially a British Guiana tree although small stands also occur in Surinam. The heartwood varies in color from light to dark olive green or nearly black. The texture is fine and uniform.

Greenheart is stronger and stiffer than white oak and generally more difficult to work with tools. The heartwood is rated as very resistant to decay and termites. It also is very resistant to marine borers in temperate waters but much less so in warm tropical waters.

Greenheart is used principally where strength and resistance to wear are required and include ship and dock building, wharves, piers, and trestles.

IROKO (*Chlorophora Excelsa* [Welw.] Benth.)

Iroko is a large tree widely distributed in tropical Africa. The heartwood varies from light to greenish yellow with occasional darker streaks. Upon exposure to light and air, it darkens to various shades of brown. The wood is without odor or taste but may have a slightly oily or waxy feel. The grain is interlocked and the texture is coarse.

The heartwood is very resistant to decay and resistant but not immune to termite attack and marine borers. The heartwood is very resistant to preservative treatment. It works fairly well in most hand and machine operations and has fairly good nail- and screw-holding properties.

Iroko resembles teak in a number of properties, but its strength values are somewhat lower.

The principal uses of iroko are in heavy construction, furniture, and boat construction.

JARRAH (*Eucalyptus Marginata* Sm.)

Jarrah occurs in a compact belt of forest about 20 miles wide that runs parallel to the coast of western Australia from the latitude of Perth about 200 miles southward. It is the only species of commercial value in the area.

The wood is hard and heavy and is reddish brown in color, although it varies from light red to very dark red when first cut. The texture is coarse, and the grain commonly is interlocked. It has good durability with respect to decay and is resistant to termites. It is comparatively easy to work with machine tools. It is a heavy wood, weighing about 51 pounds per cubic foot in the air-dry condition.

It is used where high strength and durability are required.

KHAYA or "African Mahogany"

The bulk of the khaya shipped from West Africa is *Khaya ivorensis* A. Chev., which is the most widely distributed and most plentiful species of the genus found in the coastal belt of the so-called closed or high forest. The closely allied species, *Khaya anthotheca* (Welw.) C. DC. has a more restricted range and is found further inland in regions of lower rainfall but well within the area now being worked for the export trade.

The heartwood varies from a pale pink to a dark reddish brown. The grain is interlocked, and the texture is equal to that of mahogany (*Swietenia*). The wood is very well known in the United States and large quantities are imported annually. The wood is easy to season, machines and finishes well. In decay resistance, it is generally rated below American mahogany.

Principal uses include furniture, interior finish, boat construction, and veneer.

LAUANS or "Philippine Mahogany"

The term "Philippine mahogany" is applied commercially to Philippine woods belonging to three genera — *Shorea*, *Parashorea*, and *Pentacme* (Plate XVII). These woods are usually grouped by the United States trade into "dark red Philippine mahogany" and "light red Philippine mahogany."

Plate XVII. — Lauans or "Philippine Mahogany."

The species within each group are shipped interchangeably when purchased in the form of lumber. Mayapis of the light red group is quite variable with respect to color and frequently shows exudations of resin. For this reason, some purchasers of "Philippine mahogany" specify that mayapis be excluded from their shipments.

"Philippine mahoganies" as a whole have a coarser texture than mahogany or the "African mahoganies" and do not have the dark-colored deposits in the pores.

In machining, the Philippine species appeared to be about equal with the better of the hardwoods found in the United States.

The shrinkage and swelling characteristics of the Philippine species are comparable to those found in the oaks and maples of the United States.

Principal uses include interior trim, paneling, flush doors, plywood, cabinets, furniture, siding, and boat construction. The use of the woods of the dark red group for boat building in the United States exceeds in quantity that of any foreign wood.

LIGNUMVITAE (*Guaiacum* spp.)

The principal sources of lignumvitae are the West Indies, Central America, Colombia, Venezuela, and southern Mexico.

Lignumvitae is one of the heaviest and hardest woods on the market. The wood is characterized by its unique green color and oily or waxy feel. The wood has a fine, uniform texture and closely interlocked grain. Its resin content may constitute up to about one-fourth of the air-dry weight of the heartwood.

Lignumvitae wood is used chiefly for bearing or bushing blocks for the lining of stern tubes of steamship propeller shafts. The great strength and tenacity of lignumvitae, combined with the self-lubricating properties that are due to the high resin content, make it especially adaptable for underwater usage. It is also used for such articles as mallets, pulley sheaves, caster wheels, stencil and chisel blocks, various turned articles, and brush backs.

LIMBA (*Terminalia Superba* Engl. & Diels)

Abundant supplies of limba or korina occur in West Africa and Belgian Congo (Plate XVIII).

Plate XVIII. — Limba (also known as Korina).

The wood varies in color from a gray white to creamy brown and may contain dark streaks, which are valued for special purposes. The light-colored wood is considered an important asset for the manufacture of blond furniture. The wood is generally straight grained and of uniform but coarse texture.

The wood is easy to season and the shrinkage is reported to be rather small. Limba is not resistant to decay, insects, or termites. It is easy to work with all types of tools and is veneered without difficulty.

Principal uses include interior trim, paneling, and furniture.

MAHOGANY (*Swietenia Macrophylla* King)

Mahogany ranges from southern Mexico through Central America into South America as far south as Bolivia (Plate XIX). Mexico, British Honduras, and Nicaragua furnish about 70 percent of the mahogany imported into the United States.

The heartwood varies from a pale to a dark-reddish brown. The grain is generally straighter than that of "African mahogany;" however, a wide variety of grain patterns are obtained from this species.

Among the properties that mahogany possesses to a high degree are dimensional stability, fine finishing qualities, and ease of working with tools.

The principal uses for mahogany are furniture, models and patterns, boat construction, radio and television cabinets, interior trim, paneling, precision instruments, and many other uses where an attractive and dimensionally stable wood is required.

PRIMAVERA (*Cybistax Donnell-Smithii* [Rose] Siebert)

The natural distribution of primavera is restricted to southwestern Mexico, the Pacific coast of Guatemala and El Salvador, and north central Honduras (Plate XX).

Primavera is regarded as one of the primary light-colored woods, but its use has been limited because of its rather restricted range and the relative scarcity of wild trees within its natural growing area.

The heartwood is whitish to straw yellow and in some logs may be tinted with pale brown or pinkish streaks. The wood has a very high luster.

Plate XIX. — Mahogany.

Plate XX. — Primavera.

Primavera produces a wide variety of figure patterns.

The shrinkage properties are very good, and the wood shows a high degree of dimensional stability. Although the wood has considerable grain variation, it machines remarkably well. Its durability with respect to decay resistance is rated as durable to very durable.

The dimensional stability, ease of working, and pleasing appearance recommend primavera for solid furniture, paneling, interior trim, and special exterior uses.

ROSEWOOD (*Dalbergia* spp.)

All of the true rosewoods known to cabinetmakers are various species of the genus *Dalbergia* from Asia, Madagascar, Brazil, and Central America. The wood has excellent technical properties, attractive appearance, and is usually fragrant (Plate XXI).

The heartwood of these species varies in color from black to reddish brown with black streaks or mottlings. The wood is easy to work and finishes smoothly with a high natural polish. It holds its place well in the finished items and is very durable.

The chief obstacles to a wider use of rosewood are the high cost and the fact that the trees are usually small and defective. Only the heartwood has any commercial value. A great deal of the better timber, especially that which was readily accessible, has already been utilized. Formerly used in making pianos and fine cabinets, its uses now are limited to levels, brush backs, cutlery handles, and marquetry. Principal species are Brazilian rosewood, East Indian rosewood, Honduras rosewood, Madagascar rosewood, and African blackwood, which is used primarily for the manufacture of clarinets.

TEAK (*Tectona Grandis* L. f.)

Teak occurs in commercial quantities in India, Burma, Thailand, Indo-China, and the East Indies (Plate XXII). Numerous plantations have been developed and many of these are now producing timber.

The heartwood varies from a yellow brown to a rich brown. It has a coarse texture, is usually straight grained, and has a distinctly oily feel. The heartwood has excellent dimensional stability and possesses a very high degree of natural durability.

Plate XXI. —Rosewood.

Plate XXII. — Teak.

Intrinsically, teak is one of the most valuable of all woods, but its use is limited by scarcity and high cost. Teak is unique in that it does not cause rust or corrosion when in contact with metal; hence, it is extremely useful in the ship building industry. It is currently used in the construction of expensive boats, furniture, flooring, and decorative objects.

PROPERTIES, SELECTION, AND SUITABILITY OF WOODS FOR WOODWORKING

Wise selection of wood for woodworking entails first of all the determination of the requirements of that use. These requirements vary with the quality of the articles produced and the conditions to which the articles will be subjected in service. The wood best adapted to a given use will, therefore, not always be the same. Ash and southern yellow pine furnish an example of widely different woods used successfully for the same article. Ash is used for bats for college, semiprofessional, and professional ball players. Southern yellow pine serves equally well as ash for bats for small boys of the grade-school age because for children's bats the strength and toughness requirements are not so high. The necessity for careful observation is illustrated in a mistake commonly made in selecting wood for diving boards. Decay-resistant woods are often selected because of the wetting to which the boards are subjected. Diving boards, however, usually fail mechanically in less than 2 years if they are subjected to continuous use, such as at popular public beaches. The selection of a comparatively high-priced, weak wood of high decay resistance for diving boards in preference to a low-priced strong wood of moderate or low decay resistance, as is often done, is obviously wasteful, because the purchaser is paying for decay resistance, a property of little or no importance to the use requirement.

After the requirements of use are determined it is relatively easy to check the properties of the different woods to see whether these requirements would be met. Wood for the exposed parts of most articles must be sufficiently hard to resist denting in ordinary usage. Many woods are strong enough and possess other qualities which would fit them for use in exposed parts of such articles as furniture but are barred for lack of the required hardness. Butternut is a good example of such a wood. On the other hand, the wood must not be too hard, or it will be too difficult to work.

Wood which has the requisite hardness also is sufficiently strong not to break in handling or in use, unless weakened by defects. On the other hand numerous woods, like basswood, cottonwood, chestnut, or willow, are not only too soft but too weak (unless used in comparatively large sizes) for the substantial parts of high-grade furniture. Even the stronger woods, such as oak and walnut, fail occasionally in use because of cross grain, decay, or too deep carving or mortising.

Good appearance is required in wood used for most kinds of woodworking. Many woods which otherwise would be suitable for high-class woodworking have not a sufficiently attractive figure or color to make them desirable.

Comparative freedom from warping and from excessive shrinking and swelling is essential in woods used in woodworking. The enviable reputations of mahogany and walnut are due in part to this characteristic, and the usual preference of quarter-sawed to plain-sawed lumber is based on the common experience that the quarter-sawed warps less. Changes in the dimensions of wood cannot, however, be avoided entirely. As a general rule, the heavier and harder species shrink more than the lighter and softer ones.

The fashioning of wood at the proper dryness means practically no serious shrinkage later. Wood at the time of working should therefore be seasoned to about the average moisture content that it will have in service. Proper seasoning does not necessarily mean that the lumber shall stand in piles air drying for a given number of years, but simply that it shall be dried to a proper and uniform moisture content and be free from seasoning defects and internal stresses. In the seasoning of wood the modern lumber manufacturer, with his closely-regulated dry kilns, has a distinct advantage over the old-time cabinetmaker, who has no such equipment and therefore often turned out a product which shrank, warped, or checked in use.

To work easily, glue without much difficulty, and finish well also are important from the woodworker's standpoint.

Resistance to decay is not an important factor in the selection of wood to be made up into household articles, since practically all such articles in use are too dry to be subject to decay. In fact, maple, birch, gum, and other woods which rank low in durability in damp locations are used extensively and with good results in household articles.

Appearance, style, and finishing qualities are the properties dominating the selection of woods for furniture. Ability to stay in place, nonsplitting, and good holding power for screws and nails are important requirements for woods used in concealed parts of furniture. Although the shifts from one wood to another in furniture are practically unpredictable from year to year, nevertheless large quantities of red gum, yellow-poplar, maple, chestnut, and tupelo go into furniture every year.

It is not often that one property alone controls the choice of wood for a given article. Usually it is the degree to which two or more properties are combined. Before the user can find the combination he needs for his specific purpose he must be prepared to think in terms of specific and individual properties.

In the following paragraphs the various woods are classified into three broad groups according to several important properties. The classification is based principally upon factual data obtained at the Forest Products Laboratory. No attempt has been made to draw fine distinctions between woods. Neither is it to be inferred that all woods in the same class are equally suitable.

The classification assumes equal size, equal dryness, and for strength properties equal freedom from knots and the like, as between the different kinds of wood. So far as size is concerned, in actual practice all the different kinds of softwood lumber are governed by the same standards. However, some woods, mostly eastern hemlock, eastern spruce, and northern white pine, and some southern yellow pine, are commonly cut one thirty-second of an inch fuller than the general standard for 1-inch lumber. Where such oversized lumber is also dry at the time of dressing so that subsequent shrinkage does not reduce the thickness, there is, of course, an advantage in the strength due of oversize, and the classification as given does not apply without modification. On the other hand, some boards of some woods are sold substandard, that is, three thirty-seconds of an inch under and some dimension material one-sixteenth of an inch under the standard thickness. Such differences must be taken into account in comparing the strength of species where strength is really important.

In actual practice different shipments of the same kind of lumber vary rather widely in dryness according to the source of the lumber. Some kinds of lumber run consistently drier than others because of the ease of seasoning the wood. A difference of one thirty-second of an inch in the thickness of boards and one-sixteenth of an inch in the thickness of dimension may exist due to difference in dryness at time of dressing. Regardless of the cause the fact stands out that a slight increase in size may easily compensate for inherently lower strength properties.

Hardwoods in some of their properties and uses differ substantially from softwoods. As a class they are heavier, harder, shrink more, and are tougher than the softwoods. Hardwoods and softwoods are very similar in stiffness, which means that reduced to a weight-for-weight basis the softwoods are much stiffer. In strength as a post, that is, the compressive strength endwise, and in bending strength the two groups are more directly comparable than they are in weight, toughness, and hardness, but there are more of the commercial hardwoods than of the commercial softwoods that can be rated high in bending strength. The softwoods are used principally in construction work, whereas hardwoods furnish most of the wood for implements, furniture, and other industrial uses.

Hardness is the property that makes a surface difficult to dent, scratch, or cut (fig. 7). The harder the wood, other things being equal, the better it resists wear, the less it crushes or mashes under loads, and the better it can be polished; on the other hand, the more difficult it is to cut with tools, the harder it is to nail, and the more liable it is to split in nailing. Hardness is a property that one seeks in such uses as flooring, furniture, and tool handles.

There is a pronounced difference in hardness between the springwood and the summerwood of some woods, such as southern yellow pine and Douglas-fir. In these woods the summerwood is the denser, darker colored portion of the annual-

HARDNESS

High	Intermediate	Low
Ash, black	Baldcypress	Basswood
Ash, white	Chestnut	Butternut
Beech	Douglas-fir	Cedar, northern
Birch, yellow	Hemlock, eastern	white
Cedar, eastern red	Hemlock, western	Cedar, southern
Cherry	Redwood	white
Elm, rock	Sweetgum	Cedar, westernred
Elm, soft		Cottonwood
Hackberry		Fir, balsam
Hickory, pecan		Fir, white
Hickory, true		Pine, eastern white
Larch, western		Pine, ponderosa
Locust, black		Pine, sugar
Locust, honey		Pine, western white
Maple, hard		Spruce, eastern
Maple, soft		Spruce, Engelmann
Oak, red		Spruce, Sitka
Oak, white		Yellow-poplar
Pine, southern		
yellow		
Sycamore		
Tupelo		
Walnut		

growth ring. In such woods differences in surface hardness occur at close intervals on a piece, depending on whether springwood or summerwood is encountered. In woods like maple, which do not have pronounced springwood and summerwood, the hardness of the surface is quite uniform.

The classification of a species as a hardwood or softwood is not based on actual hardness of wood. Technically, softwoods are those cut from coniferous or evergreen trees, whereas hardwoods are those cut from broad-leaved and deciduous trees. Actually, some of the softwoods are harder than some of the hardwoods, and conversely.

The strong position that a number of woods hold among carpenters for building purposes is due in part to their soft-

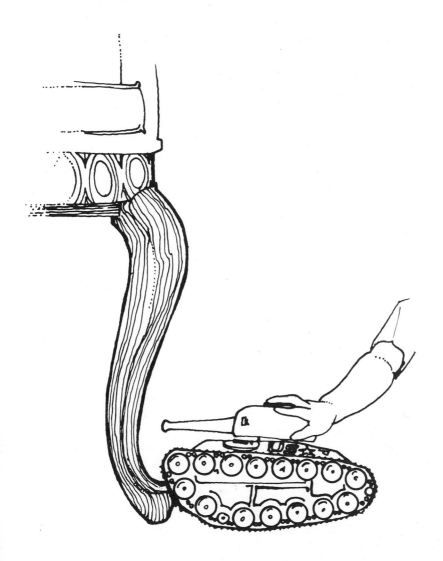

Figure 7.— Hardness is a measure of the ability of wood to resist wear.

ness and uniformity rather than to their hardness. Eastern white pine, yellow-poplar, and basswood are traditional examples. The ease with which these and other woods, such as ponderosa pine, sugar pine, and western white pine, can be cut, sawed, and nailed has put them in a high position for general use, and particularly for uses involving considerable working with machine and hand cutting tools. It is generally recognized that differences among woods in the matter of hardness are sufficiently great to have an important bearing on the choice of woods for such uses as flooring and furniture, on one hand, and for siding, millwork, and cabinets, on the other.

WEIGHT

High	Intermediate	Low
Ash, white	Ash, black	Basswood
Beech	Baldcypress	Cedar, northern
Birch,yellow	Cherry	white
Cedar, eastern red	Chestnut	Cedar, southern
Elm, rock	Cottonwood	white
Elm, soft	Douglas-fir	Cedar, westernred
Hackberry	Hemlock, eastern	Fir, balsam
Hickory, pecan	Hemlock, western	Fir, white
Hickory, true	Pine, ponderosa	Pine, eastern white
Larch, western	Pine, western white	Pine, sugar
Locust, black	Redwood	Spruce, Engelmann
Locust, honey	Spruce, eastern	
Maple, hard	Spruce, Sitka	
Maple, soft	Sweetgum	
Oak, red	Yellow-poplar	
Oak, white		
Pine, southern		
yellow		
Sycamore		
Tupelo		
Walnut		

Weight, in addition to being important in itself, is a reliable index of the strength properties of dry wood when the degree of dryness and actual sizes are the same. A heavy piece of dry wood is stronger, as a rule, than one lighter in weight whether of the same or of a different species.

Weights as commonly expressed are either the weight of the wood in the green condition or its weight in the air-dry condition. The former is its weight when cut from the living tree; the latter is the weight at which the lumber is best suited for use under the average outdoor conditions in the United States. The classification given here is based on the air-dry condition.

FREEDOM FROM SHRINKAGE AND SWELLING

High	*Intermediate*	*Low*
Cedar, eastern red	Ash, white	Ash, black
Cedar, northern white	Baldcypress	Basswood
	Cherry	Beech
Cedar, southern white	Chestnut	Birch, yellow
	Douglas-fir	Cottonwood
Cedar, westernred	Fir, balsam	Elm, rock
Pine, eastern white	Fir, white	Elm, soft
Pine, sugar	Hemlock, eastern	Hackberry
Redwood	Hemlock, western	Hickory, pecan
	Larch, western	Hickory, true
	Locust, black	Maple, hard
	Locust, honey	Oak, red
	Maple, soft	Oak, white
	Pine, ponderosa	Sweetgum
	Pine, southern yellow	Sycamore
	Pine, western white	
	Spruce, eastern	
	Spruce, Engelmann	
	Spruce, Sitka	
	Tupelo	
	Walnut	
	Yellow-poplar	

Most materials change in dimension with changes in temperature or moisture. In the case of wood, the thermal expansion is so small as to be unimportant in ordinary usage. Wood, like many other fibrous materials, shrinks as it dries and swells as it absorbs moisture. As a rule, however, much of the shrinking and swelling of wood in service is unnecessary and can be avoided by using wood that has been dried to the right moisture content.

In all kinds of wood the shrinkage or swelling in the width of a flat-grained board is nearly twice that of a quarter-sawn or edge-grained board of the same width (fig. 8). Edge-grained or quarter-sawn wood of a species having high shrinkage will therefore prove as satisfactory as flat-grain stock of the kinds with inherently lower shrinkage. Wood has practically no shrinkage or swelling lengthwise of the grain.

The classification according to the amount of freedom from shrinkage as given here does not tell the user the whole story of the shrinking and swelling of different species in service. About half of the shrinkage is "taken out" of wood in thorough air-seasoning and about two-thirds in thorough kiln-drying. The taking out of the shrinkage in the foregoing amounts is sufficient for the ordinary uses to which wood is put. Of course, the shrinkage does not stay out when moisture is reabsorbed, but the important thing is to have it taken out at the time the wood is built into a structure. The rate at which drying and shrinkage occur in different kinds of wood is very important in practical usage. A wood that has a relatively low total shrinkage may dry so slowly that, in actual practice, it commonly gets into use before the proper amount of shrinkage has been taken out. Individual pieces of some woods, such as western larch, bald-cypress, and redwood, frequently are slow to dry and therefore slow to shrink to their ultimate condition. Such pieces are liable to give a greater amount of trouble from shrinkage than the actual shrinkage values for the species indicate. This is a condition that can be controlled by making sure that such woods are thoroughly and uniformly dry prior to use. Ponderosa pine, sugar pine, northern white pine, western white pine, and the cedars give up their moisture quite readily and uniformly, and the chances of encountering shrinkage difficulties with such wood are correspondingly minimized.

The means of determining whether wood is dry enough for use is discussed on page 117.

Warping (fig. 9) is responsible for much waste in fabri-

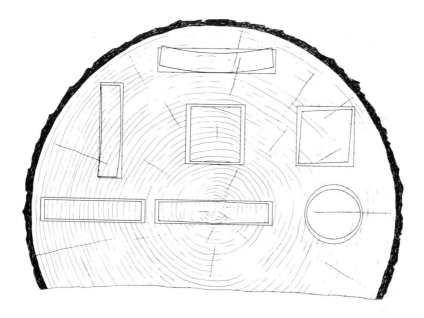

Figure 8. — *Characteristic shrinkage and distortion of flats, squares, and rounds as affected by the direction of the annual rings. Tangential shrinkage is about twice as great as radial.*

cating and for some unsatisfactory service. It is defined as: "Any variation from a true or plane surface. Warp includes bow, crook, cup, and twist." The warping of wood is closely allied with shrinkage. Lumber that is cross-grained, or is from near the central core of the trees, tends to warp when it shrinks. Warping can be reduced to a minimum by the use of quarter-sawed dry material. The combined characteristics of warping and shrinkage determine the ability of wood to stay in place. Ability to stay in place, that is, remain flat, straight, and not change size, is desired in practically all uses. It is especially important in furniture and cabinetwork. All woods require proper seasoning in order to stay in place well.

FREEDOM FROM WARPING

High	*Intermediate*	*Low*
Cedar, eastern red	Ash, black	Beech
Cedar, northern white	Ash, white	Cottonwood
	Baldcypress	Elm, soft
Cedar, southern white	Basswood	Sweetgum
	Birch, yellow	Sycamore
Cedar, westernred	Douglas-fir	Tupelo
Cherry	Elm, rock	
Chestnut	Fir, balsam	
Pine, eastern white	Fir, white	
Pine, ponderosa	Hackberry	
Pine, sugar	Hemlock, eastern	
Pine, western white	Hemlock, western	
Redwood	Hickory, pecan	
Spruce, eastern	Hickory, true	
Spruce, Engelmann	Larch, western	
Spruce, Sitka	Locust, black	
Walnut	Locust, honey	
Yellow-poplar	Maple, hard	
	Maple, soft	
	Oak, red	
	Oak, white	
	Pine, southern yellow	

Figure 9.— Warping is caused by uneven shrinkage.

The tendency of different woods to warp and twist during seasoning and incident to changes in atmospheric conditions once the wood is dry is shown in the foregoing list.

EASE OF WORKING WITH HANDTOOLS

High	Intermediate	Low
Basswood	Baldcypress	Ash, black
Cedar, northern white	Cedar, eastern red	Ash, white
	Chestnut	Beech
Cedar, southern white	Cottonwood	Birch, yellow
	Fir, balsam	Cherry
Cedar, westernred	Fir, white	Douglas-fir
Pine, eastern white	Hemlock, eastern	Elm, rock
Pine, ponderosa	Hemlock, western	Elm, soft
Pine, sugar	Redwood	Hackberry
Pine, western white	Spruce, eastern	Hickory, pecan
Yellow-poplar	Spruce, Engelmann	Hickory, true
	Spruce, Sitka	Larch, western
	Sweetgum	Locust, black
	Walnut	Locust, honey
		Maple, hard
		Maple, soft
		Oak, red
		Oak, white
		Pine, southern yellow
		Sycamore
		Tupelo

Wood in general is easy to cut, shape, and fasten with ordinary tools (fig. 10). For some purposes the difference between woods in ease of working is negligible, but for others the smoothness and facility with which it can be worked have a decided influence on the quality of the finished job. In general, along with the tendency toward splitting in nailing, warping and twisting, and the weight in handling, ease of working is of first importance to the worker. The load-carrying capacity and wear resistance of the harder and denser woods should not be

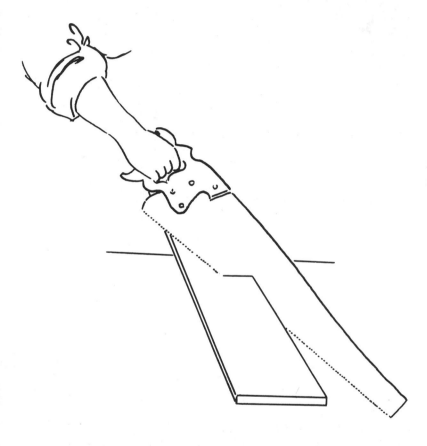

Figure 10.—Ease of working is an important consideration where hand tools are used.

sacrificed unduly for the ease of working of the softer woods, but a reasonable balance must be drawn in selecting wood for a specific use. A skilled carpenter working with lumber that is well seasoned and manufactured can get good results from even the more refractory woods, whereas an unskilled worker stands the best chance of getting good results from the easier working woods. The condition of the cutting edges of tools is of first importance because unsuitable or dull tools may lose for any species of wood the advantage it may have because of its ease of working.

Classification of the more common woods according to their working qualities is shown in the foregoing list. The classification is based on a combination of the hardness, texture, and character of the surfaces obtainable. Woods in the high class have soft, uniform texture and finish to a smooth surface, woods in the low class are hard or nonuniform in texture or less easy than high or intermediate woods to surface without chipping the grain, fuzzing, or grain raising. The intermediate class is between the groups described.

Planing (Hardwoods)

Least difficult.	*Intermediate*	*Most difficult*
Beech	Ash	Birch (sweet)
Hackberry	Basswood	Cottonwood
Magnolia	Buckeye	Elm, soft
Oak, chestnut	Chestnut	Hickory
Oak, red	Pecan	Maple, hard
Oak, white	Tupelo	Maple, soft
Sweetgum		Sycamore
Yellow-poplar		Willow

Much greater care is required with some woods than with others to obtain smooth surfaces with a planer (fig. 11). These differences can be largely eliminated by proper control of speed, moisture content, and cutting angle. High cutter-head speeds (5400 r.p.m. and 54 feet feed per minute) give better results than low speeds (3600 r.p.m. and 36 feet feed per minute). The above classification is based on the chip marks, chipped,

Figure 11. — *Control of speed, moisture content, and cutting angle are essential in planing.*

raised, and fuzzy grain that developed in planning wood at 6, 12, and 20 percent moisture content with a cabinet planer having knives set at a 30° angle and operated at the two speeds just mentioned. Good planing qualities are desired in practically all uses to which wood is put by the home woodworker.

SHAPING (HARDWOODS)

Least difficult	*Intermediate*	*Most difficult*
Birch (sweet)	Ash	Basswood
Hickory	Beech	Buckeye
Maple, hard	Chestnut	Cottonwood
Oak, chestnut	Elm, soft	Magnolia
Oak, red	Hackberry	Tupelo
Oak, white	Maple, soft	Willow
Pecan	Sweetgum	
Sycamore	Yellow-poplar	

Almost any wood makes a passable showing when shaped at a slight angle to the grain (fig. 12). It is in shaping across the end grain that the big differences between species show up. Further experiments will no doubt reveal means of improving the results with the more difficult woods. Meanwhile preliminary tests group the woods as shown above, smoothness of cut and absence of splintering or chipping being the governing considerations. The shaper used was of the standard two-knife type running at a typical commercial speed of 7,200 r.p.m.

TURNING (HARDWOODS)
Relative Yield of "Smooth" Turnings

Beech 93	Oak, red 84	Maple, soft 78
Pecan 89	Oak, white 82	Elm, soft 70
Hickory 86	Ash 81	Basswood 70
Sweetgum 86	Hackberry 79	Cottonwood . . . 70
Sycamore 85	Magnolia 79	Willow 60
Yellow-poplar . . 84	Tupelo 79	

(Modified back knife lathe: 6, 12, 20, percent moisture content.)

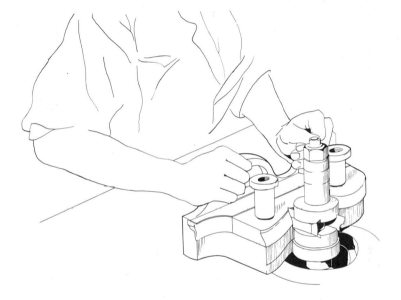

Figure 12. — Shaping is one of the more exacting machining operations.

Some of the woods, like beech and pecan, turn (fig. 13) relatively well regardless of moisture content. Other woods, like cottonwood and willow, give good turnings only if dried down to about 6 percent moisture content. In general, the heavier woods turn better than the lighter ones, and heavy pieces turn better than light pieces in the same wood. The main points considered in rating the foregoing woods as to quality of turnings were general smoothness, sharpness of detail, and occurrence of broken or chipped edges, as affecting the amount of sanding that must be done to make them acceptably smooth for use.

BENDING BREAKAGE (HARDWOODS)

Percent	*Percent*	*Percent*
Oak, white 9	Ash 36	Maple, hard 51
Oak, red 14	Beech 40	Tupelo 53
Oak, chestnut . . 18	Sweetgum 44	Cottonwood . . . 69
Magnolia 18	Maple, soft 47	Sycamore 84
Birch, sweet . . . 22	Chestnut 50	Basswood 95
Elm, soft 28	Yellow-poplar . . 51	

Most hardwoods can be bent readily into a curved form. The comparatively low toughness of softwoods as a group makes them difficult to bend without excessive breakage. The foregoing classification applies in bending hardwood squares three-fourths inch in size on a 20-inch radius without end pressure or any support on the outside of the bend (fig. 14) and without selection beyond excluding knotty, decayed, or checked pieces.

The amount of steaming and the manner in which pressure is applied are important factors in bending. However, insofar as the wood itself is concerned some kinds must be selected and handled more carefully than others. Bending breakage is an important consideration in selecting woods suitable for boat building, certain types of furniture, and other uses. The types of bending breakage are shown in figure 15.

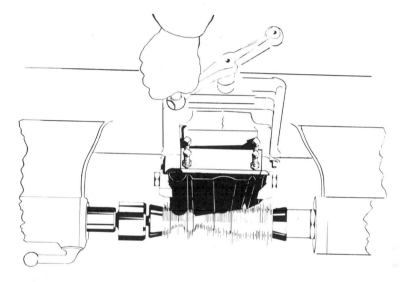

Figure 13. — *Turning is an important property in the selection of wood for furniture.*

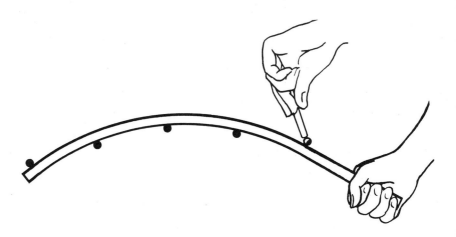

Figure 14.—*The amount of steaming and the manner in which pressure is applied are important factors in bending.*

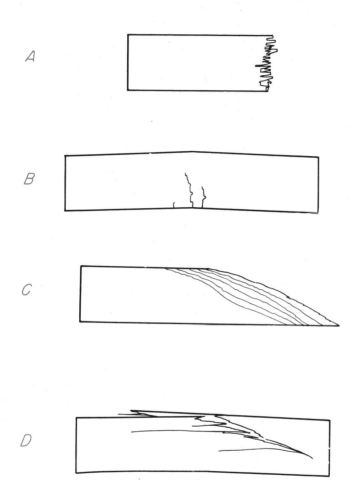

Figure 15. — Types of bending breakage. A, Brash break — the most common type in oak. B, Compression failure — sometimes found in softer woods like yellow-poplar. C, Cross grain failure — not uncommon in black gum, red gum, tupelo, and sycamore. D, Tension failure — much the most common type in ash, elm, magnolia, soft maple, and cottonwood.

NAIL HOLDING

High	*Intermediate*	*Low*
Ash, white	Baldcypress	Basswood
Beech	Chestnut	Cedar, northern
Birch, yellow	Douglas-fir	white
Elm, soft	Hemlock, eastern	Cedar, westernred
Hickory, true	Hemlock, western	Cottonwood
Larch, western	Pine, eastern white	Fir, white
Locust, black	Pine, ponderosa	Spruce, Engelmann
Locust, honey	Pine, western white	
Maple, hard	Redwood	
Maple, soft	Spruce, eastern	
Oak, red	Sweetgum	
Oak, white	Yellow-poplar	
Pine, southern		
yellow		
Sycamore		
Tupelo		

As a rule, fastenings are the weakest link in all forms of construction and in all materials; therefore the resistance which is offered by the wood itself to the withdrawal of nails is important. Usually, the denser and harder the wood the greater is the inherent nail-holding power (fig. 16). The foregoing classification, of the commercial woods according to their inherent nail-holding power, is based on tests that measured the number of pounds required to pull nails from wood.

The size, type, and number of nails have a marked effect on the strength of the joint. The resistance to withdrawal of nails increases almost directly with the diameter; that is, if the diameter of the nail is doubled the holding power is doubled, providing the nail does not split the wood when it is driven. The lateral resistance of nails increases as the 1½ power of the diameter. Of the three nails most commonly used, plain, cement-coated, and barbed, the cement-coated nail has, in well-seasoned wood, the highest holding power and the barbed nail the lowest. New or specialized types of nails are introduced on the market from time to time, some of them giving substantially improved results. One of these new nails is minutely pitted or etched in such a way as to increase the holding power even more than does the cement-coating just mentioned.

The moisture content of the wood at the time of nailing is extremely important for good nail holding. If nails are driven into wet wood they will lose about three-fourths of their full holding power when the wood becomes dry. So large is this loss that siding, barn boards, or fence pickets are very likely to become loose when nails are driven into green wood even when the best of nails and nail-holding woods are used. Barbed nails are better adapted for use with wet or poorly dried wood than either plain or cement-coated nails when for some unavoidable reason wood in such a condition must be used. The first and most important rule in obtaining good joints and high nail-holding power is to use well-seasoned wood.

The splitting of wood by nails greatly reduces their holding power. Even if the wood is split only slightly around the nail there is considerable loss in holding power. Because of hardness and texture characteristics some woods split more in nailing than do others. The heavy, dense woods, such as maple, oak, and hickory, split more in nailing than do the lightweight woods, such as basswood, spruce, and true firs. The nonuniform-textured woods, like southern yellow pine and Douglas-fir, split more than do the uniform-textured woods like northern white pine, sugar pine, or ponderosa pine. The most common means taken to reduce splitting is the use of smaller nails. The number of small nails must be increased, of course, to maintain the same gross holding power. Blunt-pointed nails are now available on the market, and sharp-pointed nails can be blunted, a handful at a time, on a grindstone or emery wheel. Blunt-pointed nails have a smaller tendency to split wood than do sharp-pointed nails. Too much blunting, however, results in a loss of holding power.

The old-fashioned cut nail with its blunt point has less tendency to split than does the modern pointed nail. Cut nails, however, do not have the holding power of the modern pointed nail.

The foregoing classification of the splitting tendencies of 23 important hardwoods is based upon the percentage of complete splits in driving 7d box nails into air-dry boards three-

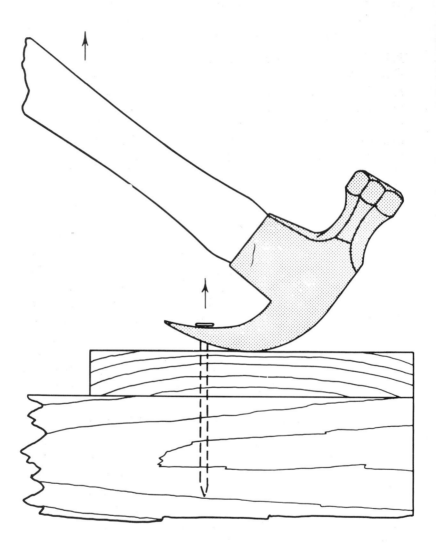

Figure 16. — Nail-holding power is the force required to start the ***direct*** *withdrawal of a nail from a piece of wood.*

eighths of an inch thick, the nails being driven within one-half inch of the ends of the boards.

SPLITTING IN NAILING (HARDWOODS)

Splits by less than 25 percent of nails	Splits by 25 to 40 percent of nails	Splits by over 40 percent of nails
Buckeye	Ash	Beech
Cottonwood	Basswood	Birch, sweet
Elm, soft	Chestnut	Hackberry
Sycamore	Magnolia	Hickory
Willow	Oak, red	Maple, hard
Yellow-poplar	Oak, white	Maple, soft
	Sweetgum	Oak, chestnut
	Tupelo	Pecan

The splitting tendencies of different kinds of wood are important factors in the selection of wood for certain uses, notably boxes and crates, and frames to which upholstery is fastened in furniture. Splitting is controllable within limits by the shape of the nail point (fig. 17), the size of the nails, and the manner in which the nails are driven. Driving a nail tends to distort the fibers next to the nail downward (fig. 18), causing a downward accumulation of stress so that splitting makes its first appearance on the under side. Danger of splitting will be

SPLITTING IN SCREWING (HARDWOODS)

Splits by 20 to 29 percent of screws	Splits by 30 to 39 percent of screws	Splits by over 40 percent of screws
Ash	Hackberry	Basswood
Cottonwood	Hickory	Beech
Elm, soft	Maple, soft	Birch, sweet
Magnolia	Oak, chestnut	Buckeye
Oak, red	Pecan	Chestnut
Oak, white	Sweetgum	Maple, hard
Sycamore	Willow	Tupelo
	Yellow-poplar	

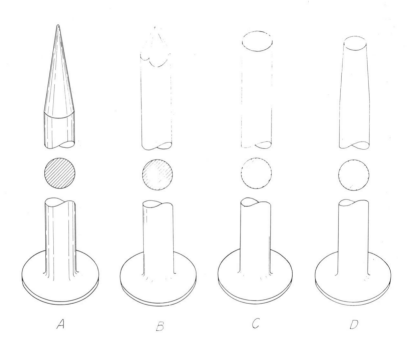

Figure 17.—Types of nail points: A, *Long and sharp;* B, *common;* C, *blunt;* D, *blunt tapered.*

reduced if nails are staggered. Boring holes for nails also reduces the danger of splitting.

With wood screws in drilled holes the tendency is for any splits that develop to start on the upper side of the board (fig. 19). The unthreaded portion just below the head exerts a wedging effect. Pronounced distortion of fibers alongside the screw is lacking. Some woods that split more readily with nails make a much better showing with screws. The foregoing classification of woods is based on the percentage of screws of various sizes causing complete splits under drastic conditions, namely, in three-eighths inch air-dry stock, the screws being driven within three-fourths inch from the end.

BENDING STRENGTH

High	Intermediate	Low
Ash, white	Ash, black	Basswood
Beech	Baldcypress	Cedar, northern
Birch, yellow	Cedar, eastern red	white
Cherry	Elm, soft	Cedar, southern
Douglas-fir	Fir, white	white
Elm, rock	Hackberry	Cedar, westernred
Hickory, pecan	Hemlock, eastern	Chestnut
Hickory, true	Hemlock, western	Cottonwood
Larch, western	Pine, western white	Fir, balsam
Locust, black	Redwood	Maple, soft
Locust, honey	Spruce, eastern	Pine, eastern white
Maple, hard	Spruce, Sitka	Pine, ponderosa
Oak, red	Sweetgum	Pine, sugar
Oak, white	Sycamore	Spruce, Engelmann
Pine, southern	Tupelo	
yellow	Yellow-poplar	
Walnut		

Bending strength is a measure of the load-carrying capacity of members that are ordinarily used in a horizontal position and rest on two or more supports (fig. 20). Examples of members in which bending strength is important are barn rafters, girders, bridge stringers, and scaffold platforms.

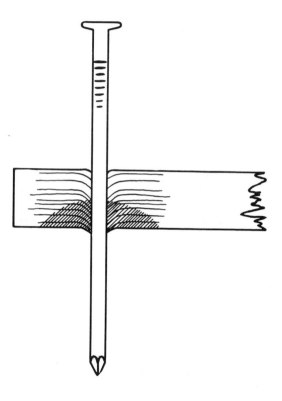

Figure 18.— Splitting in nailing makes its first appearance on the under side of the board.

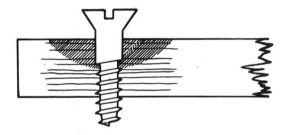

Figure 19.—Splitting in screwing makes its first appearance on the upper side of the board.

Figure 20. — Bending strength is a measure of the load-carrying capacity of beams, which are usually horizontal members resting on two supports.

Even though a wood is low in bending strength it does not necessarily follow that it is unsuited for uses where this property is one of the essential requirements. It does indicate, however, that to obtain the same load-carrying capacity larger sizes are required.

A small increase in the height of a beam produces a much greater increase in bending strength than it does in the volume. Thus, an increase of 1 inch in the height of a 10-inch beam will increase its volume 10 percent, whereas the bending strength of the beam when set on edge is increased 21 percent. An increase in the width of a beam, however, increases the volume and bending strength by the same percentage, that is, an increase of 1 inch in a beam 10 inches wide will increase both bending strength and volume 10 percent.

No simple rule can be given to determine the size of girder, board, or plank required to carry a given load. In general, it may be said that for girders, the distance between the supporting posts in feet should not be greater than the height of the girder in inches.

The softwoods classed here as high dominate the structural field. They are used for both heavy construction, such as barns and bridges, and light construction, such as dwellings and small farm structures. In heavy construction, softwoods in the intermediate class are used only occasionally. In light construction, softwoods in the intermediate class are used extensively. Their light weight and ease of working enable them to compete with the stronger woods. Woods classed as low are relatively unimportant in the structural field. They are seldom if ever used in heavy construction and only occasionally in light construction. The hardwoods in the high and intermediate classes have largely dropped out of the construction field not because they are unsuited to the use but because of their value for uses having more exacting requirements.

Stiffness is a measure of the resistance to bending or deflection under a load (fig. 21). In the floor joists of houses and in studding, stiffness is more important than actual breaking strength because it is deflection that must be reduced to the minimum in order to avoid plaster cracks in ceilings and vibration in floors. Stiffness is important also in shelving, ladder

STIFFNESS

High	Intermediate	Low
Ash, white	Ash, black	Cedar, eastern red
Beech	Baldcypress	Cedar, northern white
Birch, yellow	Basswood	Cedar, southern white
Cherry	Cottonwood	Cedar, westernred
Douglas-fir	Elm, soft	Chestnut
Elm, rock	Fir, white	Fir, balsam
Hemlock, western	Gum, red	Hackberry
Hickory, pecan	Hemlock, eastern	Maple, soft
Hickory, true	Pine, western white	Pine, eastern white
Larch, western	Redwood	Pine, ponderosa
Locust, black	Spruce, eastern	Pine, sugar
Locust, honey	Sycamore	Spruce, Engelmann
Maple, hard	Tupelo	
Oak, red	Yellow-poplar	
Oak, white		
Pine, southern yellow		
Spruce, Sitka		
Walnut		

rails, beams, ax handles, and long, slender columns. Whereas stiffness is of great importance. in floor joists the actual advantages of using a species of relatively high stiffness will be lost if the members are not fully dry at the time of installation so that the fastenings, bracing, and bridging hold well. Well-seasoned, well-bridged, and straight joists of a kind of wood that is relatively low in stiffness may be counted upon to give better results than a simply inherently stiff wood. If the wood is properly dry and the installation is good, however, species differences with respect to stiffness are important.

Differences in stiffness between various woods may be compensated for by changing the size of members. Height and length of members have a greater effect on their stiffness than on other strength properties. A change of one thirty-second of an inch in the thickness of a standard 25/32-inch board produces a change of 12 percent in the stiffness of the board laid

Figure 21.—Stiffness is a measure of the resistance to deflection, and relates particularly to beams.

flat in a floor. A 10-inch joist has about one-fourth more wood in it than an 8-inch joist, but set on edge in a building it is more than twice as stiff.

The various woods are here classified in accordance with their stiffness. Softwoods classed as high and as intermediate dominate the uses where stiffness is the most important requirement. When woods classed as low are used where stiffness is desired, it is because other properties are more important. The woods classed as high have the highest stiffness, but they are heavier and harder than those in the intermediate class. Light. weight is quite commonly desired in combination with stiffness. The softwoods meet this requirement much better than the hardwoods, and softwoods in the intermediate class are often chosen in preference to those classed as high because the weight of the latter excludes them.

Stiffness is little affected by such defects as knots, checks, and shake. In light building construction, therefore, material of the sound, though knotty, grades may be used to good

STRENGTH AS A POST

High	Intermediate	Low
Ash, white	Baldcypress	Ash, black
Cedar, eastern red	Beech	Basswood
Cherry	Birch, yellow	Cedar, northern
Douglas-fir	Cedar, westernred	white
Hickory, pecan	Elm, rock	Cedar, southern
Hickory, true	Elm, soft	white
Larch, western	Fir, white	Chestnut
Locust, black	Hemlock, eastern	Cottonwood
Locust, honey	Hemlock, western	Fir, balsam
Maple, hard	Oak, red	Hackberry
Pine, southern	Oak, white	Maple, soft
yellow	Pine, western white	Pine, eastern white
Redwood	Spruce, eastern	Pine, ponderosa
Walnut	Spruce, Sitka	Pine, sugar
	Sweetgum	Spruce, Engelmann
	Sycamore	Yellow-poplar
	Tupelo	

advantage for joists and studs because stiffness is more important than breaking strength in these items.

Compression members are generally square or circular in cross section, usually upright, supporting loads that act in the direction of the length (fig. 22). Strength as a post is an essential requirement of supports for root cellars, for storage bins, and for posts in similar heavy construction where the length is less than 11 times the smallest dimension. It is not important in fence posts which carry no loads. The size requirements of posts, with the smallest dimension less than one-eleventh of the length, is determined in small buildings by bearing area, stiffness, and stability rather than by actual compressive strength. These requirements necessitate the use of posts large enough to carry much greater actual compressive loads than are ever placed upon them. No great consideration need therefore be given to compressive strength endwise in selecting a wood for small houses. Where exceptionally heavy loads are involved, as in supports for bins or root cellars, consideration should be given to compressive strength. Even where compressive strength is an important requirement, the woods in any of the classes may be safely used, provided the lower strength of the woods in the intermediate and low classes is compensated for by the use of timber of larger cross-sectional area.

When the length is greater than 11 times the smallest dimension, the slenderness has increased to such an extent that stiffness has become an important factor in determining the load-carrying ability and the comparisons with respect to compression strength are of no special significance. Unbraced supports in machinery-storage sheds and barns with an attached lean-to are generally so slender that they should be judged by their stiffness rather than by their compressive strength.

Toughness is a measure of the capacity to withstand suddenly applied loads (fig. 23). Hence, woods high in shock resistance are adapted to withstand repeated shocks, jars, jolts, and blows, such as are given ax handles, baseball bats, and bowling pins. The heavier hardwoods, like hickory, yellow birch, the oaks, maple, and ashes, are so much higher in shock resistance than the toughest of the softwoods that the hardwoods are used almost exclusively where an exceptionally tough wood is required.

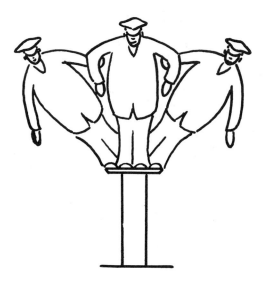

Figure 22. — *Strength as a post is a measure of the ability of wood to withstand loads that tend to shorten the piece.*

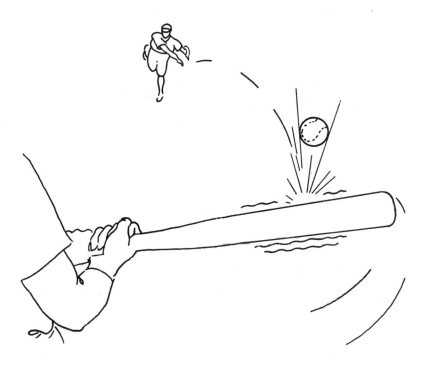

M 31718 F

Figure 23. — *Toughness is a measure of the capacity to withstand suddenly applied loads.*

None of the softwoods grouped here is classed as high in toughness, and only two hardwoods, basswood and yellow-poplar, fall in the low class. The woods classed as high completely dominate the uses where toughness is the outstanding requirement, and hickory dominates the high class.

TOUGHNESS

High	Intermediate	Low
Ash, black	Baldcypress	Basswood
Ash, white	Cedar, eastern red	Cedar, northern
Beech	Cherry	white
Birch, yellow	Chestnut	Cedar, southern
Elm, rock	Cottonwood	white
Elm, soft	Douglas-fir	Cedar, westernred
Hackberry	Hemlock, eastern	Fir, balsam
Hickory, pecan	Hemlock, western	Fir, white
Hickory, true	Larch, western	Maple, soft
Locust, black	Pine, southern	Pine, eastern white
Locust, honey	yellow	Pine, ponderosa
Maple, hard	Pine, western white	Pine, sugar
Oak, red	Redwood	Spruce, Engelmann
Oak, white	Spruce, eastern	Yellow-poplar
Walnut	Spruce, Sitka	
	Sweetgum	
	Sycamore	
	Tupelo	

Toughness is a desirable property in uses other than those in which it is an outstanding requirement. Tough woods give more warning of failure than do nontough woods. It is, therefore, a factor in beams and girders where heavy loads are applied and where failure will result in loss of life or heavy property damage. The warning given by tougher woods often makes it possible to reinforce a member and thus prevent a complete failure. Softwoods in the intermediate class give warning of failure by detectable deflection and cracking noise, while softwoods in the low class, in which the size of knots, pitch pockets, and the like are relatively large, break more suddenly at low deflections.

DECAY RESISTANCE OF HEARTWOOD

High	Intermediate	Low
Baldcypress	Douglas-fir	Ash, black
Cedar, eastern red	Elm, rock	Ash, white
Cedar, northern white	Elm, soft	Basswood
Cedar, southern white	Larch, western	Beech
Cedar, westernred	Locust, honey	Birch, yellow
Chestnut	Pine, southern yellow	Cottonwood
Locust, black	Sweetgum	Fir, balsam
Oak, white		Fir, white
Redwood		Hemlock, eastern
Walnut		Hemlock, western
		Hickory, pecan
		Hickory, true
		Maple, hard
		Maple, soft
		Oak, red
		Spruce, eastern
		Spruce, Engelmann
		Spruce, Sitka
		Sycamore
		Tupelo
		Yellow-poplar

Conflicting opinion and absence of adequate test data preclude a definite rating of the decay resistance of the soft pines; high decay resistance should not be relied upon when soft pines are used untreated.

Every material has its characteristic way of deteriorating under adverse conditions. With wood it is decay. Wood, of course, will last indefinately if kept continuously dry. Fortunately, most wood is used in dry situations and therefore not in danger of decay. It is only in certain parts of buildings that decay resistance is of importance, such as where wood is damp or in contact with the ground. Hence, in order to protect wood from decay, make sure that the wood is dry when put in place and kept dry in service; or where moisture is certain to get in, as from contact with the soil, or liable to get in because drainage or ventilation is poor, use either the heartwood of a decay-resistant species or wood that has been given a good preservative treatment.

The different kinds of wood are classified here in accordance with their natural decay resistance. This classification applies solely to the heartwood, because sapwood of all species in the untreated condition has low decay resistance. Furthermore, this classification deals only with averages, and exceptions frequently occur because of variations in conditions of exposure, because of variations in the wood itself, and because of differences in the kinds of fungi that cause the decay. The classification has application only where the wood is used under conditions that favor decay. The wood of all classes will last indefinitely if kept continuously dry.

PROPORTION OF HEARTWOOD

High	*Intermediate*	*Low*
Cedar, northern white	Baldcypress	Ash, black
	Beech	Ash, white
Cedar, southern white	Cedar, eastern red	Basswood
	Cherry	Birch, yellow
Cedar, westernred	Elm, rock	Cottonwood
Chestnut	Elm, soft	Fir, white
Douglas-fir	Fir, balsam	Hackberry
Larch, western	Hemlock, eastern	Maple, hard
Locust, black	Hemlock, western	Maple, soft
Redwood	Hickory, pecan	Pine, ponderosa
	Hickory, true	Pine, southern
	Locust, honey	yellow
	Oak, red	Spruce, eastern
	Oak, white	Spruce, Engelmann
	Pine, eastern white	Spruce, Sitka
	Pine, sugar	Tupelo
	Pine, western white	
	Sweetgum	
	Sycamore	
	Walnut	
	Yellow-poplar	

Selection of wood for use untreated where the decay hazard is high must take into consideration the heartwood content. When the sapwood of the tree is characteristically narrow, as it is in the woods rated here as "high," the lumber runs high in heartwood content even without special selection. When, however, the sapwood is characteristically wide, as in woods rated as "low," and even in those rated "intermediate," the commercial run of lumber contains considerable sapwood. To obtain decay-resistant lumber, even in the species classed as "high" in decay resistance, it is necessary to eliminate the sapwood by special selection. Specially selected building lumber, sold in what is commercially known as "all-heart" grades, is procurable in baldcypress, redwood, western redcedar, Douglas-fir, and southern yellow pine (fig. 24).

AMOUNT OF FIGURE

High	*Intermediate*	*Low*
Ash, black	Beech	Basswood
Ash, white	Birch, yellow	Cedar, northern
Baldcypress	Cedar, eastern red	white
Chestnut	Cedar, westernred	Cedar, southern
Douglas-fir	Cherry	white
Elm, rock	Fir, balsam	Cottonwood
Elm, soft	Fir, white	Pine, eastern white
Hackberry	Hemlock, eastern	Pine, ponderosa
Larch, western	Hemlock, western	Pine, sugar
Locust, black	Hickory, pecan	Pine, western white
Locust, honey	Hickory, true	Tupelo
Oak, red	Maple, hard	
Oak, white	Maple, soft	
Pine, southern	Redwood	
yellow	Spruce, eastern	
	Spruce, Engelmann	
	Spruce, Sitka	
	Sweetgum	
	Sycamore	
	Walnut	
	Yellow-poplar	

The choice of wood for woodwork that is to be varnished or waxed is usually based largely upon the character of the figure in the wood. Figure is due to different causes in different

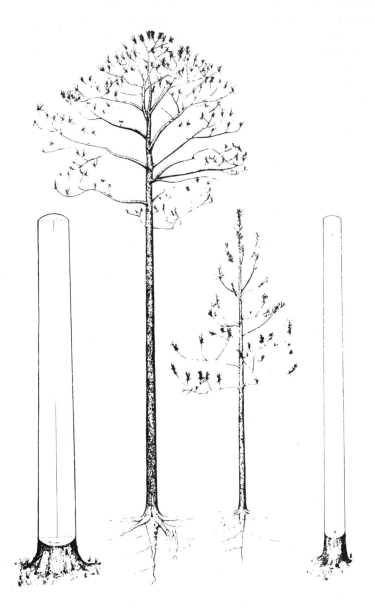

Figure 24.— Relative amounts of heartwood (shaded area at center of trunk) and sapwood in a young and mature southern yellow pine.

woods. In woods like southern yellow pine and Douglas-fir it results from the contrast within the growth rings; in others, such as oak, beech, or sycamore, it results from the flakes or rays in addition to the growth rings; in maple, walnut, and birch it results from wavy or curly grain; and in red gum it results from deposited coloring matter. Except where the figure in wood results from flakes or rays, the figure is more pronounced in plain-sawed lumber than in quarter-sawed. Figure resulting from wavy or curly grain or from deposited color does not occur in all lumber of a given species but only in lumber from occasional logs. To be certain of getting figured lumber in maple, walnut, or red gum special selection is necessary.

The color of wood has a decided influence on the figure. Stains, however, are so commonly and easily applied to practically all woods that the natural color is usually not of the first consideration except where a very light color is desired.

Woods classed here as high are highly figured, and an ordinary commercial run will have a pronounced figure. Those classed intermediate have more modulated figures and it sometimes requires special selection to obtain the desired figure. Woods classed as low woods are seldom satisfactory where figure is desired.

None of the common woods has sufficient odor to prevent its entirely satisfactory use in building construction or cabinet work. It is only for food containers that odor and taste have to be taken into account. When green, all woods have some odor and will impart a woody taste to very susceptible foods. Many woods, however, which have a disagreeable odor when green have practically no odor or taste after they are dried. The principal objection to odor and taste in wood is that they contaminate food, especially butter and cheese, in contact with the wood. The aromatic odor of the cedars is desirable in some uses, such as clothes closets and chests. The woods classed as high have practically no odor or taste when dry and have been found by test or experience to be suitable for use in contact with foods that absorb odors. The woods classed as low have strong resinous or aromatic odor and are unsuited for use where they come into direct contact with food that absorbs odors. Woods in the intermediate class, while they cannot be

Freedom from Odor and Taste When Dry

High	*Intermediate*	*Low*
Ash, white	Baldcypress	Cedar, eastern red
Basswood	Cherry	Cedar, northern
Beech	Chestnut	white
Birch, yellow	Cottonwood	Cedar, southern
Elm, rock	Locust, black	white
Elm, soft	Locust, honey	Cedar, westernred
Fir, balsam	Sweetgum	Douglas-fir
Fir, white		Larch, western
Hackberry		Pine, eastern white
Hemlock, eastern		Pine, ponderosa
Hemlock, western		Pine, southern
Maple, hard		yellow
Maple, soft		Pine, sugar
Spruce, eastern		Pine, western white
Spruce, Engelmann		
Spruce, Sitka		
Tupelo		
Yellow-poplar		

used in contact with very susceptible foods, like butter, do not have the strong odor and taste of the aromatic and resinous woods.

Surface Characteristics of Lumber

Lumber is purchased on account of its appearance as well as on account of its working characteristics and strength properties. The appearance is dependent largely on the grade, and there is some degree of uniformity in the appearance of the same grade in different woods. Different woods are more uniform in appearance in the select grades than in common grades because most knots, pitch pockets, and the like are eliminated from the select grades. In the common grades, however, where knots and similar surface features are allowable, there are characteristic differences in the same grade of different woods. These differences affect the appearance of the wood and at times its suitability for a use.

Knots

A knot is a branch, or limb, embedded in a tree that has been cut through in the process of lumber manufacture. If the sawed section of a knot is oval or circular it is known as a round knot. A branch, or limb, which in the process of lumber manufacture has been sawed in a lengthwise direction is known as a spike knot (fig. 25, *A*). A sound, tight knot is solid across its face, fully as hard as the surrounding wood, shows no signs of decay, and is so fixed by growth or position that it will firmly retain its place in the piece.

Knots are further classified as intergrown or encased (fig. 25, *B* and *C*). As long as a limb remains alive, there is continuous growth at the junction of the limb and the trunk of the tree, and the resulting knot is called intergrown; after the limb has died, additional growth on the trunk encloses the dead limb and an encased knot results. The encased knot and the fibers of the trunk are not continuous, and consequently the distortion of the grain around the knot is less than for intergrown knots. Encased knots and knot holes are accompanied by less cross grain than are intergrown knots and hence have no more effect on the bending strength of lumber than do intergrown knots.

Knots affect in three different ways any piece in which they occur:

1. *Appearance*. Except for knotty finish, knots are considered objectionable from the standpoint of appearance, but the smaller and fewer they are the less objectionable. Sound tight knots present the best appearance.

2. *Strength*. Knots reduce the strength of lumber according to their number, size, quality, and position in the piece. Contrary to popular opinion a knot hole reduces the strength less than an intergrown knot of equal size because the wood fibers are distorted more around an intergrown knot than around the hole. However, lumber used for woodworking is not graded primarily for strength and this factor is therefore not of determining importance.

3. *Tightness*. For many uses tightness is important and in tightness intergrown knots rank first. They are so fixed by growth that they cannot come out under ordinary conditions. If intergrown knots are large, however, they sometimes check

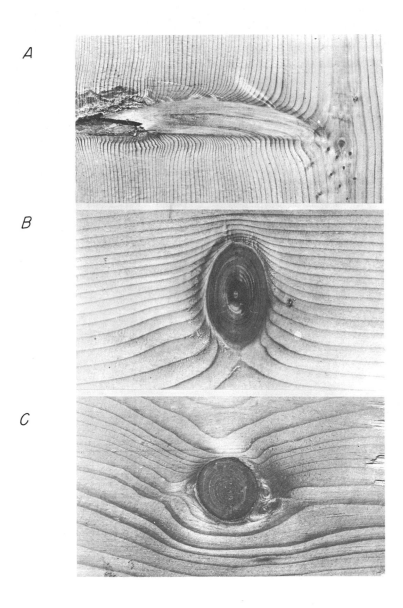

Figure 25. — A, *Spike knot;* B, *intergrown knot;* C, *encased knot.*

in drying, and especially if located on the edge of the piece they sometimes break in machining. Knots that are completely encased may or may not loosen and drop out eventually depending on growth, position, dryness, size, and species. Symmetrical encased knots and those running through the board at nearly right angles are more likely to loosen than irregular ones or knots passing through the board obliquely.

Because shrinkage accompanies the drying of lumber it has a loosening effect on the encased knots. It happens, then, that encased knots which are tight in a green board sometimes become loose when the board is dry. No doubt knots of all sizes shrink about the same amount relatively, but the absolute shrinkage of large knots is greater and therefore they are more likely than small knots to loosen enough to fall out in drying.

Number of Knots
(Commercial lumber)

Least	*Intermediate*	*Most*
Ash, black	Beech	Cedar, eastern red
Ash, white	Douglas-fir	Cedar, northern
Baldcypress	Elm, rock	white
Basswood	Elm, soft	Fir, balsam
Birch, yellow	Fir, white	Larch, western
Cedar, westernred	Hemlock, eastern	Pine, eastern white
Cherry	Hemlock, western	Pine, sugar
Chestnut	Hickory, true	Pine, western white
Cottonwood	Locust, black	Spruce, eastern
Hackberry	Locust, honey	Spruce, Engelmann
Hickory, pecan	Maple, hard	
Maple, soft	Pine, ponderosa	
Oak, red	Spruce, Sitka	
Oak, white		
Pine, southern		
yellow		
Redwood		
Sweetgum		
Sycamore		
Tupelo		
Walnut		
Yellow-poplar		

The tendency of knots to loosen is to some extent a species characteristic, that is, some woods are naturally more tight knotted than others.

Size of Knots
(Commercial Lumber)

Large	*Intermediate*	*Small*
Cedar, westernred	Ash, black	Cedar, eastern red
Chestnut	Ash, white	Cedar, northern
Hackberry	Baldcypress	white
Hickory, pecan	Basswood	Cottonwood
Hickory, true	Beech	Fir, balsam
Oak, red	Birch, yellow	Larch, western
Oak, white	Cherry	Pine, eastern white
Pine, southern	Douglas-fir	Pine, western white
yellow	Elm, rock	Spruce, eastern
Redwood	Elm, soft	Spruce, Engelmann
	Fir, white	Tupelo
	Hemlock, eastern	
	Hemlock, western	
	Locust, black	
	Locust, honey	
	Maple, hard	
	Maple, soft	
	Pine, ponderosa	
	Pine, sugar	
	Spruce, Sitka	
	Sweetgum	
	Sycamore	
	Walnut	
	Yellow-poplar	

Knots are by far the commonest defect in all lumber, comprising on the average from 70 to 80 percent of all defects in the common grades.

Woods vary considerably in the average size of knots. This has, of course, been recognized by the trade in referring to one wood as fine-knotted or to another wood as coarse-knotted. A species which is conspicuous for either fine or coarse knots shows the characteristic consistently grade after grade. Obviously the larger the knot the greater its effect both on service-ability and on appearance.

The average of the maximum and minimum diameters is used in measuring the size of knots in the grading of lumber. The foregoing classification of woods according to size of knots is based on this method of measurement.

Pitch

Pitch is an accumulation of resin in the wood cells in a more or less irregular patch. It often accumulates in the wood near a burn or mechanical injury. The pitch has the effect of making the wood more decay resistant but more difficult to paint or varnish, depending of course upon the degree of pitch present. The select grades of lumber allow only a small amount of pitch. In some species special grades, such as export and pitchy clears, take much of the most pitchy lumber.

Pitch pockets are the commonest type of pitch defects and occasional small ones are allowed in the select grades of lumber. Doubtless they have a slight weakening effect, but the most serious objection is that liquid pitch sometimes runs out of the board in use. This is not very common, however, as many of the pockets are dry, or contain hard pitch, or are practically emptied in the kiln drying. Pitch pockets (fig. 26, *A*) are confined to the pines, spruces, Douglas-fir, tamarack, and western larch.

The number of pitch defects in the foregoing species are classified as follows:

Number of Pitch Defects
(Commercial Lumber)

Least	*Intermediate*	*Most*
Larch, western	Douglas-fir	Pine, southern
Pine, eastern white	Pine, ponderosa	yellow
Pine, sugar		
Pine, western white		
Spruce, eastern		
Spruce, Engelmann		
Spruce, Sitka		

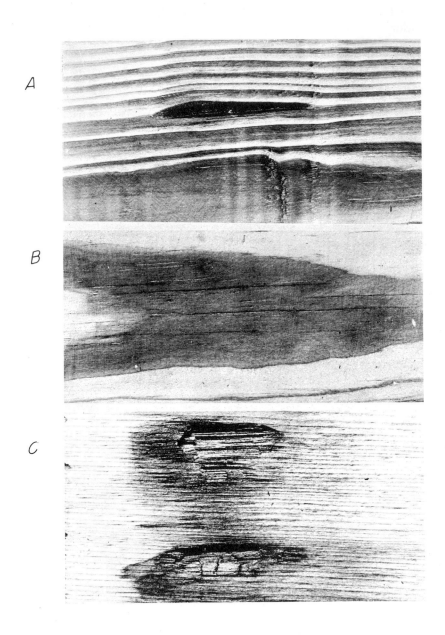

Figure 26. — A, *Pitch pocket;* B, *check;* C, *decay.*

The size of pitch defects is given in the following classification:

Size of Pitch Defects
(Commercial Lumber)

Large	Intermediate	Small
Pine, southern yellow	Douglas-fir	Larch, western
	Pine, ponderosa	Pine, eastern white
	Spruce, Sitka	Pine, sugar
		Pine, western white
		Spruce, eastern
		Spruce, Engelmann

Number of Miscellaneous Defects

Most	Intermediate	Least
Beech	Ash, black	Basswood
Chestnut	Ash, white	Cedar, eastern red
Elm, soft	Baldcypress	Cedar, northern white
Hemlock, eastern	Birch, yellow	Cedar, westernred
Hickory, pecan	Douglas-fir	Cottonwood
Larch, western	Elm, rock	Maple, soft
Pine, western white	Fir, balsam	Redwood
	Fir, white	Sweetgum
	Hackberry	Tupelo
	Hemlock	Walnut
	Hickory, true	Yellow-poplar
	Locust, black	
	Locust, honey	
	Maple, hard	
	Oak, red	
	Oak, white	
	Pine, eastern white	
	Pine, ponderosa	
	Pine, southern yellow	
	Pine, sugar	
	Spruce, eastern	
	Spruce, Engelmann	
	Spruce, Sitka	
	Sycamore	

Miscellaneous Defects

The term "defect" as used in this publication and as defined in American lumber standards means "Any irregularity occurring in or on wood that may lower some of its strength, durability, or utility values." The following classification of the number of miscellaneous defects therefore includes checks (fig. 26, *B*), shake, decay (fig. 26, *C*), splits, and manufacturing defects.

The miscellaneous defects may be classified as to size as follows:

Size of Miscellaneous Defects

Large	*Intermediate*	*Small*
Beech	Ash, black	Basswood
Elm, soft	Ash, white	Cedar, eastern red
Fir, white	Baldcypress	Cedar, northern
Hemlock, eastern	Birch, yellow	white
Hickory, pecan	Chestnut	Cedar, westernred
	Douglas-fir	Cottonwood
	Elm, rock	Gum, red
	Fir, balsam	Larch, western
	Hackberry	Maple, soft
	Hemlock, western	Pine, sugar
	Hickory, true	Pine, western
	Locust, black	white
	Locust, honey	Tupelo
	Maple, hard	Walnut
	Oak, red	Yellow-poplar
	Oak, white	
	Pine, eastern white	
	Pine, ponderosa	
	Pine, southern	
	yellow	
	Redwood	
	Spruce, eastern	
	Spruce, Engelmann	
	Spruce, Sitka	
	Sycamore	

MOISTURE CONTENT OF WOOD
AT DIFFERENT HUMIDITIES

Wood kept for any length of time under fixed atmospheric conditions tends to come to a definite moisture content, the percentage being dependent upon the humidity conditions prevailing. For instance, lumber placed out of doors but protected from rain and snow in the northern states eventually retains about 12 percent moisture; at certain places in the arid Southwest or in heated buildings it retains only 4 to 6 percent moisture.

Since any absorption or loss of moisture in seasoned wood causes swelling or shrinking, wood should be brought to nearly the proper moisture content before being manufactured into delicate parts or put in any service where the retention of exact shape is important.

The installation of wood at the proper dryness means practically no serious shrinkage later. Wood at the time of use should therefore be seasoned to about the average moisture content that it will have in service. At the time of use the moisture content of wood to be used indoors should be in most parts of the United States between 5 and 10 percent; in the damp southern coastal regions, where the humidity is high, the moisture content should be between 8 and 13 percent; and for the dry southwestern region, where the humidity is low, the moisture content should be between 4 and 9 percent (fig. 27).

SEASONING OF LUMBER
Moisture in Wood

The moisture in wood, commonly called "sap", may for all practical purposes in the drying of wood be considered as water alone. Table 2 gives some moisture-content values for green heartwood and sapwood of various woods. The values shown may be considered average, and considerable variation from these values in individual trees and single boards may be expected, particularly in sapwood.

Sawmills cutting softwoods generally grade their products at the time of sawing. With few exceptions timbers, dimension, and low-grade lumber are sent to the yard for air seasoning

Table 2. — *Average moisture content for green heartwood and sapwood of 20 varieties of woods*

Woods	Average moisture content	
	Heartwood *Percent*	Sapwood *Percent*
Hardwoods		
Ash, white	38	40
Beech	53	78
Birch, yellow	68	71
Elm, soft	95	92
Maple:		
Soft	60	88
Hard	58	67
Softwoods		
Douglas-fir	36	117
Fir, lowland white	91	136
Hemlock:		
Eastern	58	119
Western	42	170
Pine:		
Loblolly	34	94
Lodgepole	36	113
Longleaf	34	99
Ponderosa	40	148
Red	31	135
Shortleaf	34	108
Redwood	100	210
Spruce:		
Engelmann	54	167
Sitka	33	146
Tupelo	50	61

or are shipped green, whereas the upper grades intended for interior finish, cabinet work, and flooring are kiln dried because of the use requirements. At certain mills some of the dimension and lower grades are partially kiln dried to hasten the seasoning process, to reduce the susceptibility to stain and decay, and to obtain the benefit of lowered freight charges. Sawmills cutting

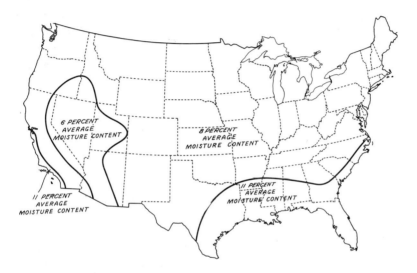

Figure 27. — *Recommended moisture-content averages for woodwork used* **indoors** *in various parts of the United States.*

hardwoods commonly classify for size and grade at time of sawing and then send all stock to the air-seasoning yard. Ultimately, hardwood stock must be kiln dried before remanufacture, since it is used mostly where a relatively low moisture content is required, as in cabinet work, interior finish, flooring, and furniture.

Air Seasoning

The principal advantages of air-seasoned over green wood are: Reduction in weight, with a resulting decrease in shipping costs; reduction in the shrinkage, checking, honeycombing, and warping occurring in service; decrease in the tendency for blue stain and for other forms of fungi to develop; reduction in liability to some forms of insect attack; increase in strength; and improvement in the capacity of the stock to hold paint.

Kiln Drying

Among the advantages over air seasoning that result from kiln drying are the following: Greater reduction in weight, and consequently in shipping charges; reduction in moisture content to any desired value, which may be lower than that obtainable through air seasoning; reduction in drying time below that required in air seasoning; and the killing of any stain or decay fungi or insects that may be in the wood.

Seasoning Defects

Material practically free of seasoning defects in the higher grade of lumber is assured by adherence to approved grading rules on the part of the manufacturer and knowledge of the material and its grades on the part of the user. Defects that sometimes develop in seasoning may be classified into two main groups: (1) Those caused by uneven shrinkage which include checks, honeycomb, warp (cup, bow, crook, and twist, fig. 28), loosening of knots, and collapse, and (2) those caused by the action of fungi, which cause molds, stains, and decay. Chemical brown stain, frequently known as yard or kiln brown stain, may also occur in some softwoods. It is a yellow to dark-brown discoloration and is apparently caused by the oxidation of water-soluble materials in the wood.

The defects enumerated under (1) and (2) can be largely eliminated by proper practice in either air seasoning or kiln drying. Too rapid drying will cause such defects as checking, honeycombing, and warping, whereas too slow drying under favorable temperatures will cause stain or decay. When defects occur the amount permitted varies with the grade of lumber as specified in the grading rules of the various lumber associations.

Honeycombing and collapse are more common in hardwoods than in softwoods and are more likely to occur during kiln drying than during air seasoning.

Moisture Content of Seasoned Lumber

The trade terms "shipping-dry", "air-dry", and "kiln-dried", although widely used, have no specific or agreed meaning with respect to quantity of moisture. The wide limitations of these terms as ordinarily used are covered in the following statements, which, however, are not to be construed as exact definitions:

Shipping-dry lumber. —Lumber that is partially air-dried to reduce freight charges and may have a moisture content of 30 percent or more.

Air-dry lumber. — Lumber exposed to the air for a sufficient length of time to reduce its moisture content to within a range from 6 percent, as in summer in the arid Southwest, to 24 percent, as in the winter in the Pacific Northwest. For the United States as a whole the minimum moisture-content range of thoroughly air-dry lumber is 12 or 15 percent, and the average is somewhat higher.

Kiln-dried lumber. — Lumber of the upper grade softwoods and upper and lower grade hardwoods intended for general use that has been kiln-dried so that it will ordinarily have a moisture content of 6 to 8 percent. Lower grade, kiln-dried softwood lumber is likely to have a moisture content of 15 to 22 percent.

Because the suitability of wood for certain purposes depends so much on the correct moisture content, specific values for the particular uses should be stated in the specifications. The importance of suitable moisture-content values is being recognized, and provisions covering them are now incorporated in some grading rules. It should be noted, however, that the moisture-content values in the general grading rules may or may not be suitable for a specific use, and if not, a special moisture-content provision should be made in the specifications.

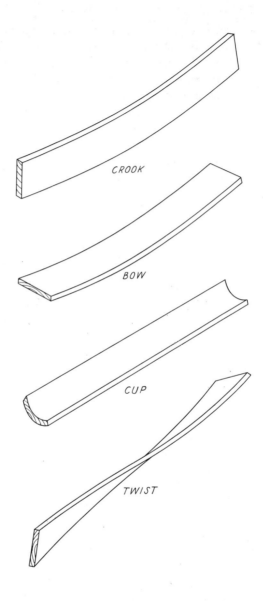

Figure 28. — Various kinds of warp.

How to Tell When Wood Is Dry

Regardless of how experienced he is, no man can tell simply by a visual inspection, by lifting it, or by the feel of the wood, whether it is adequately dried. How then can he tell when lumber is adequately seasoned? A rough check can be made rather simply. Select a half dozen flat or plain-sawed boards from various parts of the lumber pile and cut a sample from each. The sample should measure 1 inch along the grain and be cut so as to include the entire width of the board. It should be cut at least a foot from the end of the board. Trim the sample so that it will measure exactly 6 inches in width and place it in a warm, dry place — on top the furnace, in the warming oven, or on a radiator — and leave it 48 hours or until it ceases to shrink, then measure the 6-inch dimension to determine how much it has shrunk. If the wood is classed as low in freedom from shrinkage, it should not shrink more than one-eighth of an inch if it is to be used for interior trim or finish, nor over twice that amount (one-fourth of an inch) if it is to be used for framing, coverage, or where it is exposed to the weather. Woods classed as intermediate in freedom from shrinkage, should not shrink over three thirty-seconds of an inch, and woods classed as relatively high in freedom from shrinkage should not shrink over one-sixteenth of an inch if they are to be used for interior trim, finish, or floors, nor over twice that amount (one-eighth of an inch) if they are to be used exposed to the weather.

For lumber under 6 inches wide use 3-inch samples. The shrinkage limits should be half those for 6-inch samples. Edge-grain or quarter-sawed lumber shrinks only about one-half as much as plain-or flat-sawed lumber and if it is not possible to obtain a flat-grain sample, an edge-grain sample may be used, in which event the shrinkage should not be over half that shown for flat grain. It is best, however, not to use edge-grain samples or samples shorter than 6 inches; not only are they more difficult to measure, but they do not give so reliable an indication of the adequacy of seasoning.

If it is desirable to measure the adequacy of seasoning more accurately than is possible by the method just described, it can be done by determining the moisture content of the wood and comparing the results with data available on moisture-content requirements for different uses and different climatic conditions. This involves cutting the 1-inch sections from the boards, weighing them accurately, drying them to a constant weight in an oven at 214° to 221° F., reweighing, and then computing the moisture content in percentage by dividing the loss in weight by the oven-dry weight. This method is a standard by which degree of dryness is expressed for technical and commercial purposes.

Electric Moisture Meters

Electric moisture meters are convenient instruments for rapidly inspecting wood for dryness. Two types of electric moisture meters are on the market — a resistance type (fig. 29) and a radio-frequency type (sometimes called high frequency) shown in figure 30. Both types come in various styles and sizes, but within each type the operating principles are the same. Specific instructions for using each meter are supplied by the manufacturer.

LUMBER STORAGE

In general, when lumber is dried to, say, 5 to 8 percent moisture content as for cabinet work, furniture, and flooring, it will, if not properly stored, absorb moisture from the air even though protected from rain and snow. If the lumber is solid piled, the ends of the boards will absorb more moisture than the unexposed surfaces. The result is a variation in width along the length of each board. Such a variation in width leads to difficulty in gluing or fitting the boards. Further, if such boards are machined to a uniform width and immediately glued or fitted, they will subsequently undergo changes in dimension that are liable to result in an unsatisfactory product.

To obtain the best results it is necessary to store the stock so that it will not undergo undesirable changes in moisture content. If the stock has a moisture content of 6 percent, it will remain unchanged if stored in a room in which the temperature is 70° F. and the relative humidity is about 30 percent. When circumstances are such that means are not available for controlling temperature and relative humidity, considerable benefit may be had by open-piling the stock on 1- by 1½-inch

Figure 29. — *Two models of resistance-type moisture meters and two types of needle electrodes. The electrodes are interchangeable on the meters.*

Figure 30. — *Radio-frequency type of moisture meter showing the top view,*
A, and the bottom side, B. The electrodes shown are for rough-sawn lumber.

cross pieces in a moderately heated room. This practice will permit a reasonably uniform distribution of moisture within the boards, and reduce any tendency to warp.

Grades and Sizes of Lumber

A large tree when sawed into lumber yields boards of widely varying quality. Lumber grades divide the product of the tree into several parts each having a relatively narrow range in quality which enables each user to buy the quality that best suits his use and purpose.

This grade breakdown, of course, cannot be made fully uniform as between kinds or species of wood. Some species characteristically grow in such a way that they have relatively few but large knots; others relatively many but small knots. Some grow with the knots widely spaced; in others they are fairly close together. Some produce pitch pockets or diffused pitch; others produce no pitch. All species contain some decay in the trees and logs, but the species vary somewhat as to the form.

Yields of any given quality of lumber often differ widely in different species. In practice, therefore, two grades that are described separately in grading rules are sometimes combined in one species and sold separately in another. Some of the grades described in rule books are not made by all manufacturers, and some are made in very small volume.

For such reasons, it is often said that the grading of lumber is not an exact science and probably never can be. Also, it is impossible to say with mathematical accuracy that a given grade of one kind of lumber is the exact equal of another, or differs by a certain percentage.

Lumber manufacturers and dealers have used these grading rules and periodically improved them over a long period of years. While not the essence of simplicity, the whole system of lumber grades becomes clear with reasonable study and experience.

Different Types of Grades

The uses of lumber are such that three different systems of lumber grading are required.

1. Yard lumber grades for general building purposes, where the piece is to be used as a whole.

2. Factory and shop lumber grades, where the lumber is to be cut up in further manufacture.

3. Structural material of relatively large dimension where the piece is to be used as a whole and where strength factors are definitely appraised independently of appearance factors.

The bulk of softwood lumber is produced as yard lumber. The factory and shop lumber classification accounts for the bulk of the hardwood lumber, and 3 to 4 percent of the softwood lumber produced is also in this category. Another 10 to 15 percent of softwood lumber is produced as structural material, together with a very small amount of hardwood lumber. Texture, straightness of grain, rate of growth, heartwood content, density, and similar properties pertaining to the clear wood are usually not taken into account in lumber grades. There are certain exceptions; for example, in certain special use grades of structural timber, density and straightness of grain are grading criteria; and in a few species there are provisions relative to heartwood content in yard-lumber grades as well as special-use grades.

All commercial species are covered by the grading rules and size standards of a particular association or grading bureau, which in the case of softwood lumber is a regional manufacturer's association; in the case of hardwood lumber there is but one national association. In a few cases, a softwood species growing in more than one region is graded under rules of two different associations. There is great advantage to the purchaser, whether large or small, to buy according to these association grades rather than to attempt to buy according to his own individual specifications unless the requirements are actually very unusual. Occasionally a departure from the standard grade provision is necessary to cover unusual requirements. This is best handled as an exception to a standard grade rather than as an entirely special grade.

Grading rules and size standards issued by the various lumber associations may be obtained from your local lumber dealer.

PAINTING AND FINISHING WOOD

The principal reason for coating woodwork is usually

improvement and maintenance of appearance. Immediate reasons for coating wood for appearance are:

(1) Paint or enamel is opaque and therefore conceals the grain and color of the wood, substituting a color, sheen, and texture of its own.

(2) Varnish, lacquer, oil, or wax is transparent. When it saturates the fibers of wood near the surface it reveals the beauty of the grain more fully because the light penetrates farther into the wood before it is reflected back to the eye.

(3) Stain without varnish or lacquer changes the color of wood without greatly altering its sheen or texture.

Final considerations in coating wood for appearance are:

(1) Unless protected by moisture-retardant coatings, wood exposed to the weather becomes dull gray in color; smoothly planed surfaces become rough and cracked; boards tend to cup, twist, and pull loose from their fastenings; short boards may split in two; snug joints are loosened; and straight, parallel lines are disarranged. Durable coatings adequately maintained prevent such weathering.

(2) Uncoated interior wood surfaces are porous enough to absorb liquids quickly, to stain and spot readily, and to hold dirt tenaciously. Nonporous coatings or coatings that tend to shed liquids protect wood from discoloration and present a surface easily cleaned.

Ordinary paints and varnishes are not effective as preservatives against fungous decay. Fortunately those parts of buildings that are customarily kept painted are not, as a rule, subject to much hazard of decay by wood-destroying fungi.

Paint is chosen for exterior woodwork more often than any other coating; it is much more durable than varnish or other transparent coating and usually affords more effective protection against weathering of the wood (fig. 31). Exterior enamel may be used in place of paint where a smoother, harder, and more wear-resistant coating is needed, and the surface may be washed at intervals to keep it clean. It is best to limit the use of enamels to surfaces that are accessible enough to be easily repainted.

Figure 31. — A good example of protection against weathering afforded by paint. After many years of service only the painted letters on this sign resisted erosion.

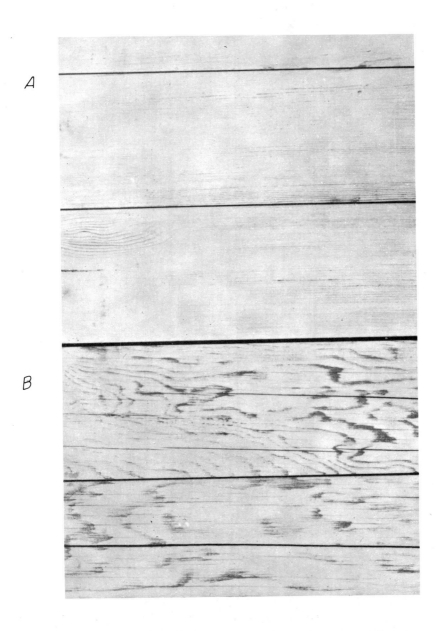

Figure 32. — Edge grain (A) *holds paint better than flat grain* (B). *Both panels are of the same kind of wood, paint, and age of paint coating.*

PAINTING CHARACTERISTICS OF WOOD

The same painting procedure and kind of paint are suitable for painting all native softwoods (conifers) and the native hardwoods that have relatively small vessels (pores). Hardwoods with relatively large vessels require a wood filler before painting or varnishing.

PAINT HOLDING (SOFTWOODS)

High	*Intermediate*	*Low*
Baldcypress	Fir, balsam	Douglas-fir
Cedar, northern white	Fir, white	Larch, western
Cedar, southern white	Hemlock, eastern	Pine, southern yellow
Cedar, westernred	Hemlock, western	
Pine, eastern white	Pine, ponderosa	
Pine, sugar	Spruce, eastern	
Pine, western white	Spruce, Engelmann	
Redwood	Spruce, Sitka	

The advantage that lies in being able to produce a change and variety of effects by the painting of wood can be realized with fullest economy by taking into account three factors, namely, (1) the kind of paint, (2) the circumstances of its application, and (3) the kind of wood. The first two factors are discussed later; only the third factor is dealt with at this point. The different kinds of wood vary considerably as to their painting characteristics, particularly for outdoor exposure. The principal softwoods are classed here according to their ability to hold paint under exposure to the weather. The dominant factor controlling the ability of a softwood to hold paint is the width of its bands of summerwood; on wide bands of summerwood paint tends to flake off at a comparatively early age.

Paint holds better on edge-grained or quarter-sawed pieces than it does on flat-sawed pieces (fig. 32). Knots in both the white and yellow pines do not retain paint so well as the sound knots of the cedars, hemlocks, white fir, or western larch. Among flat-grained boards, the bark side (the side nearest the bark of the log) is more satisfactory to paint than the pith side (fig. 33).

Figure 33. — A, *flat-grained board painted on the bark side showing a satisfactory coating;* B, *flat-grained board painted on pith side showing paint failure as a result of the grain shelling out. This panel is of the same kind of wood, paint, and age of paint coating as* A.

FILLING POROUS HARDWOODS BEFORE PAINTING

For painting purposes the hardwoods may be classified as follows:

Hardwoods with large pores: Hardwoods with small pores:

Ash	Alder, red
Butternut	Aspen
Chestnut	Basswood
Elm	Beech
Hackberry	Cherry
Hickory	Cottonwood
Khaya	Magnolia
Mahogany	Maple
Oak	Sweetgum
Sugarberry	Sycamore
Walnut	Yellow-poplar

Birch has pores large enough to take wood filler effectively when desired but small enough, as a rule, to be painted satisfactorily without filling.

Hardwoods having small pores may be painted with ordinary house paints in exactly the same manner as softwoods. In paint holding alder, aspen, basswood, cottonwood, magnolia, and yellow-poplar may be classed as intermediate, and beech, birch, gum, and maple as poor. For hardwoods with large pores the usual priming coat paint should be replaced with a wood filler, which is a paste consisting of pigment, chiefly ground quartz, mixed with linseed oil and a paint drier. Even when filled in this way the hardwoods with large pores are classed as poor in paint holding. Ability to hold paint, however, is important only for exterior painting because on interiors paint ordinarily lasts indefinitely unless it is worn through by purely mechanical abrasion.

Filler is necessary on woods having large pores because paint applied by brush or spray gun does not fill the pores properly. Without filler the pores not only appear as depressions after the painting has been finished but also act as centers from which disintegration of the coating sets in.

Drying of Paint on Softwoods

The time required for a coating of paint to dry — that is, to harden — usually depends almost entirely on the composition of the paint, the intensity of sunlight, and the temperature and relative humidity of the atmosphere. The drying is retarded, however, if the wood is wet when painted; its moisture content should not exceed 20 percent. On wet redwood or bald-cypress, priming-coat paint may remain liquid for days, especially when the paint is one containing little or no white lead or zinc sulphide pigment. On air-dry redwood paint hardens as rapidly as on any other wood. On air-dry cypress in the absence of sufficient sunlight paint may take longer than usual to harden. Cypress boards that contain much more than the average amount of the oily extractive material characteristic of cypress may retard the hardening of paints lacking white lead or zinc sulphide even when the boards are reasonably dry unless the drying takes place in strong sunlight.

Effect of Extractives in Wood on Paint Behavior

In general, the substances in wood have much less effect on paint behavior than has been commonly supposed. They are far less important than the width of the bands of summerwood.

Distinction must be made between piny resins, which are characteristic of pines but occur also in other softwoods, and other extractives.

Piny resins consist of a solid rosin and a volatile liquid such as turpentine. They affect paint unfavorably by exuding through coatings, leaving unsightly encrustations. Exudation is minimized by thorough seasoning of the lumber to drive out the turpentine, rendering the resin less mobile. Much longer seasoning is necessary to remove turpentine than to remove moisture. The piny resins may also be responsible for the fact that paints containing zinc oxide fail somewhat more rapidly on the pines than they do on other softwoods having bands of summerwood of similar width.

Other substances in wood may have a favorable effect on the durability of paint. There is evidence that such is the fact with extractives in redwood and southern cypress, although colored extractives in redwood and red cedar that are soluble in water may exude through coatings, if the wood beneath the coatings becomes very wet; under normally dry conditions these discolorations do not occur.

APPLICATION OF PAINT

Wood should not be painted when it is wet. As long as there is no free water present, however, the moisture content is of minor importance; wood painted at 16- to 20- percent moisture content holds paint slightly longer than wood painted at 10-percent moisture content. Paint dries very slowly at low temperatures; painting should therefore not be done at times when the temperature is likely to fall below 40° F. When there is danger of dew or frost at night application of paint should cease several hours before sunset. In clear warm weather coatings of paint can be applied within 24 hours of each other if necessary, but it is better practice to allow at least 2 to 3 days. On the other hand, it generally is inadvisable to allow more than 1 or 2 weeks to elapse between successive coats.

On new wood surfaces or on painted surfaces on which the old coating has not yet become deeply cracked, paint may be applied by brush or spray gun with equally serviceable results. Over old coatings that have passed well into the fissure or the flaking stage of paint deterioration, however, sprayed paint may not prove so durable as brushed paint.

The conventional procedure in painting new wood surfaces calls for the application of three coats of paints, a priming coat, second coat, and finish coat. Usually the three coats are made of the same kind of paint except for differences in proportions of pigments, linseed oil, and turpentine, but the current trend is toward the use of special paints for priming coats. Much painting of new wood is now done with only two coats, but this practice frequently leads to unsatisfactory results. When properly done 2-coat painting is practicable, but it requires much more skillful workmanship than 3-coat painting.

Painting Outside Wood Surfaces

By following a few simple, tried-and-tested procedures, the average homeowner can do a good job of painting his house.

Step 1 - Water-Repellent Preservative Treatment

Protect wood against the entrance of rain and heavy dew before painting by applying a water-repellent preservative solution. A water-repellent preservative solution gives wood the ability to shed liquid water. It can do this because of the wax-like material it contains. By repelling the water, it fights decay and stain by denying the decay and stain fungi the moisture they need to live. It also reduces water damage to the wood, such as the excessive swelling and shrinkage that leads to checking and cracking. In addition, by protecting the wood from water damage, a water-repellent preservative also protects the paint applied to the wood from blistering, cracking, and peeling, or from other abnormal paint behavior that is induced by outside water penetration. Water-repellent preservative also contains poison that kills fungi that try to live in the wood. This is usually penta (pentachlorophenol). In areas where decay is a problem, the homeowner should keep in mind that some woods, such as the heartwood of redwood and western redcedar, are more resistant to decay than other woods.

A water-repellent preservative of good quality may be made as follows:

	Percent (by weight)
Paraffin wax	1.0
Pentachlorophenol	5.2
Hydrogenated methyl ester of rosin	9.6
Pine oil	5.0
Mineral spirits	79.2
	100.0

Hydrogenated methyl ester of rosin is available as a trade name item. It has good solubility for pentachlorophenol and is, therefore, an effective antiblooming agent. It discourages recrystallization of the pentachlorophenol on the wood surface as the solvents leave the wood. It also contributes to the water repellency of the solution. Among resins that might be used are ester gums, petroleum resins, and tall oil esters.

There are two ways of providing protection with water repellents.

1. Use lumber treated by the manufacturer and retreat cut ends on the job by brushing on the solution.

2. Treatment can be applied by brushing or dipping on the job. Care should be taken to brush well into lap and butt joints. Allow 2 warm, sunny days for adequate drying of the treatment before painting.

Step 2 - Priming

For the first or prime coat on wood, use a linseed oil-base paint free of zinc-containing pigments. Apply to a thickness of 1.5 to 2 mils or 0.0015 to 0.002 inch. Beginning painters tend to thin and spread paint out too thinly. For best results, follow the spreading rates recommended by the manufacturer. Prime new wood or weathered oil-base painted surfaces with an oil-base primer when the second coat is to be an exterior emulsion or latex paint.

Step 3 - The Finish Coats

The following points should be kept in mind for best results:
1. Use a high-quality paint.
2. Apply two topcoats. A total of three coats (primer and two topcoats) should result in an optimum thickness of 4-1/2 to 5 mils. A two-coat paint job usually lasts about 3 years, but a three-coat paint job should last 6 to 7 years.
3. To avoid intercoat peeling of paint, apply topcoats within 2 weeks after the primer.
4. To avoid temperature blistering, do not apply oil-base paints on a cool surface that will be heated by the sun within a few hours. Follow the sun around the house.
5. To reduce the wrinkling and flatting of oil-base paint, do not paint late in the evenings of cool spring and fall days when heavy dews frequently form.

REPAINTING

The fundamental factor in good paint maintenance is to repaint at the right time. Neglect of repainting results in damage that cannot be satisfactorily repaired by mere application of paint. Warped and checked boards are not restored by paint, and a badly broken old coating cannot be covered smoothly without first removing it entirely which is an expensive operation.

Those who are willing to repaint often to maintain the

best possible appearance may do their repainting at some time
during the chalking stage of paint deterioration. They should
have the dirt washed off thoroughly and only one substantial
coat of paint applied.

Those who wish to repaint as infrequently as is consistent
with good maintenance usually wait for the coating to begin
to break up by cracking, crumbling, or flaking before repainting.
They should not wait too long — the first noticeable development of flaking marks a good time to repaint. Two coats are
then advisable and are usually necessary if crumbling or flaking
has begun. Any loosened parts of the old coating should be
removed with a putty knife, wire brush, or sandpaper. Conspicuous spots of bare wood should be touched up with priming-
coat paint. Two full coats of paint should then be applied.

If repainting is neglected until long after flaking sets in,
the surface may present a difficult and uncertain problem in
repainting unless the old paint was one that stands neglect well.
The safest procedure may be to burn off the old coating completely and repaint with three coats as for new wood.

In the maintenance of a paint over a long period it is
advantageous to adhere to one type of paint, at least for all
paintings after the first one. Changing the type of paint at each
time of painting builds up a coating of varying composition
with the danger that uncertainties in behavior may be encountered.

INTERIOR FINISHING

Interior finishing differs from exterior chiefly in that
interior woodwork usually requires much less adequate protection against moisture and that more exacting standards of appearance and a greater variety of effects are expected. Good
interior finishes should last much longer than exterior paint
coatings, but no interior finish should ever be used out of doors.

Opaque Finishes

Interior surfaces may, if desired, be painted with the
materials and by following the procedures recommended for
exterior surfaces. As a rule, however, smoother surfaces, better
color, and a more lasting sheen are demanded for interior wood-

work, and therefore enamels rather than paints are employed. These finishes differ from paints in that linseed oil is replaced partly or entirely by bodied oils or by varnishes in order to make a coating that does not show brush marks and presents a harder surface with a desired degree of gloss. They may also be made of nitrocellulose lacquers or synthetic resins and drying oils that dry much more rapidly than oleo-resinous enamels. Unless made with expensive pigments of extraordinary opacity, such as titanium dioxide or zinc sulphide, enamels are less opaque than paints of the same color because they cannot be made with so large a proportion of pigment.

Before enameling, the wood surface must be made extremely smooth. Imperfections, such as planer marks, hammer marks, and raised grain, are accentuated by enamel finish. Raised grain is especially troublesome on flat-grain surfaces of the heavier softwoods because the hard bands of summerwood are sometimes crushed into the soft springwood in planing and later are pushed up again when the wood changes in moisture content. It is helpful to sponge softwoods with water, allow them to dry thoroughly, and then sandpaper them lightly with sharp sandpaper before enameling. In new buildings woodwork should be allowed adequate time to come to its equilibrium moisture content before finishing.

Hardwoods having large pores must be filled with wood filler before applying the priming coat. For all woods the priming coat may be white-lead paint mixed according to directions for exterior priming-coat paint, or special priming paints made for that purpose may be used. Knots in the white pines, ponderosa pine, or southern yellow pine should be shellacked after the priming coat is dry. A coat of shellac is sometimes necessary also over the white pines and ponderosa pine to prevent discoloration of light-colored enamels by colored matter apparently present in the resin of the heartwood of these woods. One or two coats of enamel undercoat are next applied; this should completely hide the wood and should also present a surface that can easily be sandpapered smooth. For best results the surface should be sandpapered before applying the finishing enamel, but this operation is sometimes omitted. After the finishing enamel has been applied it may be left with its natural gloss or rubbed to a dull finish.

EMULSION PAINTS FOR EXTERIOR WOOD SURFACES

An emulsion paint is a paint made by combining the pigments with resin particles which have been dispersed or emulsified in water. Such paints are sometimes called latex, rubber-base, water-thinned, or water-base paints. The promising emulsion paints for exterior use on wood are either of the acrylic-resin type or vinyl-resin type.

Some Advantages of Emulsion Paints

1. Thinned with water — easy cleanup.
2. Moisture blister resistant.
3. Brushes on easily.
4. Resists fading.
5. Can be applied on a damp surface.
6. Cleanliness — dirt resistant.
7. Fast drying.
8. Drys to a "flat" finish that does not emphasize defects on the surface.

Some Disadvantages of Emulsion Paints

1. Requires three coats (one oil-base primer and two top-coats) for repainting weathered oil-base paints.
2. Requires oil-base primer for painting new wood to reduce likelihood of extractive staining.
3. Must be formulated with a fungicide to resist mildew.

General Recommendations for Painting With Emulsion Paints

1. Putty cracks and nail holes, seal knots with knot sealers, and calk open joints.
2. Use an oil-base primer on new wood or when repainting a weathered oil-base paint.
3. Spot prime all putty, calking, and rust spots around nails.
4. Sand glossy spots with sandpaper when repainting.
5. Brush chalky surfaces and wash dirt, especially oily dirt, from the surfaces before painting with primer.
6. Apply one oil-base prime coat and two emulsion-type topcoats when painting new wood or weathered oil-base paint. Emulsion topcoat can be applied directly over weathered emulsion paint.

7. Hot, dry surfaces should be sprinkled with water before painting.

8. Do not apply emulsion paints if the temperature is below 50° F.

Transparent Natural Finishes

There are many good ways of applying transparent finishes to either hardwoods or softwoods. Most finishing consists in some combination of the following fundamental operations: Staining, filling, sealing, surface coating, rubbing, and polishing. Before finishing, planer marks and other blemishes of the wood surface that would be accentuated by the finish must be removed.

Both softwoods and hardwoods are often finished without staining, especially if the wood is one with a pleasing and characteristic color. When used, however, stain often provides much more than color alone because it is absorbed unequally by different parts of the wood and therefore accentuates the natural variations in grain. With hardwoods such emphasis of the grain is usually desirable; the best stains for the purpose are dyes dissolved either in water or in oil. The water stains give the most pleasing results but raise the grain of the wood and require an extra sanding operation after the stain is dry. "Nongrain-raising" stains are now available that often approach the water stains in clearness and uniformity of color. With softwoods, stains color the springwood more strongly than the summer-wood, reversing the natural gradation in color in a manner that is often garish. Pigment-oil stains, which are essentially thin paints, are less subject to this objection than are other stains and are therefore more suitable for softwoods.

Hardwoods having large pores must be filled before a smooth varnish or lacquer coating can be applied. If a smooth coating is not desired, however, filling is optional. The filler may be transparent and without effect on the color of the finish or it may be colored to contrast with the surrounding wood. Usually colored filler is darker than the rest of the wood.

FOREST PRODUCTS LABORATORY NATURAL FINISH

An increasing number of house owners, especially those having houses with western redcedar and redwood siding, would like to use a finish that preserves the natural color and grain figure of the wood. The commercially available clear finishes are so short-lived, however, that they must be renewed at intervals of from 1 to 2 years.

A modified semitransparent oil-base stain was therefore developed at the Forest Products Laboratory in response to mounting demands from house owners for a more durable and reliable natural finish. It was formulated to overcome the more serious shortcomings inherent in natural finishes of the film-forming type that were available to house owners.

Test results indicate that one application of the finish on planed surfaces of bevel siding of redwood and western redcedar fully exposed to the weather should last 3 years before renewal. On protected areas, the finish has lasted a year or two longer. The finish should last longer on siding that receives some shelter from trees, neighboring houses, or wide roof overhang than on siding fully exposed to the weather.

The finish can be made in a variety of red and brown colors. Three colors that are well suited for use on siding are cedar, dark redwood, and light redwood.

Composition

The formulas for batches of slightly less than 5 gallons of the FPL natural finish in three colors are given in the following tabulation:

Table 3. — *Forest Products Laboratory Natural Finish*

Ingredients to make slightly less than 5 gallons of finish	Quantity of ingredient for —		
	Cedar color	Light redwood color	Dark redwood color
Paraffin wax . . . . lb.	1.0	1.0	1.0
Zinc stearate . . . . oz.	2.0	2.0	2.0
Turpentine or paint thinner gal.	1.0	1.0	1.125
Penta concentrate, 10:1 . . gal.	.5	.5	.5
Boiled linseed oil . . . . . . gal.	3.0	3.0	3.0
Burnt sienna in oil, Fed. Spec. TT-P-381, color 3B . . . . pint	1.0	2.0	.333

Raw umber in oil, Fed. Spec. TT-P-381, color 3D . . . . pint	1.0	None	.333
Indian red iron oxide in oil, Fed. Spec. TT-P-381, color 6B . . . . pint	None	None	.667

By varying the proportions of the burnt sienna and raw umber colors-in-oil, other shades can be obtained to suit individual preferences. The raw umber produces a dark brown, burnt sienna gives a red, and Indian red iron oxide produces a darker red. These colors-in-oil contain the very durable iron oxide pigments. If they conform to the minimum requirements of Federal Specification TT-P-38-1, "Pigments-in-Oil, Tinting Color," the finish will be durable. Few pigments of other kinds possess the durability of the iron oxide pigments. The finish can be made with other colors; but if so, it will usually prove less durable. Likewise, use of a smaller amount of colors-in-oil than is specified in the formula will lower the durability of the finish, even though the colors-in-oil conform to Federal Specification TT-P-381. Increasing the amount of pigments will make the finish less transparent and darker in color, but at the same time will improve the durability.

The boiled linseed oil, turpentine or other paint thinner, and colors-in-oil can be purchased at a paint store; the penta concentrate at a paint store, lumber yard, or a mail order house; the paraffin wax at the grocery store; and the zinc stearate at the drug store.

"Penta" is an abbreviation commonly used for pentachlorophenol. It is a widely used preservative and is added to the finish to protect it from mildew. Penta concentrate 10:1 is a solution that consists of about 40 percent by weight of industrial penta in a suitable solvent. It is dark in color. When the concentrate is used in the amount specified in the natural finish formula, a 5-gallon batch of the finish contains about 1.9 pounds of penta.

How The Finish Is Prepared

If proper care is exercised, the house owner himself can prepare the FPL finish, although it might be better to have a paint manufacturer or painter do it, since they are more experienced with such materials. Some paint manufacturers have included the finish in their regular lines.

To prepare the FPL finish, pour the gallon of turpentine or paint thinner into a 5-gallon pail or open-top can. Put the paraffin and zinc stearate in the top unit of a double boiler and place it over the lower half containing boiling water. Continue to heat the contents over a low flame. Stir the paraffin and zinc stearate until a uniform mixture results. Slowly pour the mixture into the turpentine or paint thinner, stirring vigorously while it is being added.

Caution: Turpentine and paint thinner are volatile flammable solvents. Their concentrated vapors should not be breathed or exposed to sparks or flames that can ignite them. Vigorous stirring should therefore accompany the addition of the hot paraffin mixture to prevent excessive heating of the turpentine or paint thinner to a temperature where it could ignite. It is safer to add the hot mixture outdoors or in an open garage or porch rather than in a closed room in the house.

When the turpentine or paint thinner solution has cooled to room temperature, add the ½ gallon of pentachlorophenol concentrate, and follow with the linseed oil. Then stir in the colors-in-oil, a little at a time, until the mixture is uniform. It is then ready for use.

How The Finish Should Be Applied

A single application of the FPL natural finish is recommended. On a smooth surface, such as the planed face of bevel siding, a gallon will cover 400 to 500 square feet. More than one application on such a surface may cause nonuniform appearance, with glossy and dull spots.

On a rough surface, such as the unplaned or sawed face of bevel siding, a a gallon should cover 200 to 250 square feet.

The finish has been used with satisfaction over other penetrating natural finishes that have weathered until they need renewal. If the finish penetrates well into the previously finished surface, it should dry to a low luster within 24 hours during good drying weather. If the finish does not penetrate well, it will dry slowly with numerous glossy areas and probably will not be so durable as it is on new wood. Varnish films should be thoroughly removed before applying the finish. A previously finished surface can be tested by applying the finish on a few small inconspicuous areas of siding that have received the greatest protection from the weather, such as on the north side of a house or just below a wide roof overhang on any side.

Where The Finish Is Properly Used

The finish has been formulated in shades of red and brown to match reasonably well the colors of the heartwood of such species of wood as redwood, western redcedar, and Philippine mahogany. It may not be quite so durable on other common siding species, but it should serve well on them. The finish was made low in hiding power to let the grain of the wood show through it. For this reason, the grain and color of the wood contribute to the final appearance of the finished wood. It is well to apply the finish on trial samples of siding to see if the color effects are satisfactory.

The Forest Products Laboratory natural finish was developed for siding and is best suited to this use. It is not suitable for interior surfaces nor will it provide sufficient protection from the weather for exterior millwork, such as frames, window sash, and doors. Such items need the protection given by paint. The finish, however, has been used with satisfaction on such wood items as fences and lawn furniture, but because they are often exposed to the weather more fully than siding, they may need refinishing more often. The finish is not considered suitable for porch floors or marine use.

Limitations Of The Finish

The FPL natural finish is rather slow in drying; a day of good drying weather is generally required for it to dry thoroughly. The wax in the finish also may interfere with subsequent painting, if it is ever desired. Laboratory refinishing tests, however, demonstrate that it can be painted over with house paints after as little exposure to the weather as 1 year. Where the finish is protected from the weather, as immediately under an overhang, it should be thoroughly scrubbed with a paint thinner or some other wax solvent before putting the paint over it.

To avoid lap marks, the finish should be applied by brushing with the grain of the wood for the full length of the board or course of siding without stopping for more than 5 minutes. The finish also should be stirred frequently during application to maintain uniform suspension of the pigments.

Advantages Of The Finish

Among the advantages of this finish are good color retention, good durability, and low cost of initial application and maintenance. Evidence to date indicates it should last approximately 3 years and should simply wear or erode away, thus presenting a very easy surface to refinish.

SEALER

Sealer is used to prevent absorption of subsequent surface coatings and to prevent the bleeding of some stains and fillers into surface coatings, especially lacquer coatings. Shellac is the oldest type of sealer. Varnish can be used as a sealer but is not so effective as shellac.

Surface Coatings

Surface coatings may be of wax, shellac, varnish, or nitro-cellulose lacquer. Wax provides a characteristic sheen without forming a coating of sensible thickness and without greatly enhancing the natural luster of the wood. Coatings of a more resinous nature, especially shellac and varnish, accentuate the natural luster of some hardwoods and seem to permit the observer to look down into the wood to a certain extent. Shellac applied by the laborious process of French polishing probably achieves this impression of depth most fully, but the coating is easily marred by water and is expensive. Rubbing varnishes made with resins of high refractive index for light are nearly as effective as shellac. Lacquers have the advantage of drying rapidly and forming a hard surface but require more applications than varnish to build a lustrous coating.

Varnish and lacquer usually dry with a highly glossy surface. To reduce the gloss the surfaces may be rubbed with pumice stone and water or polishing oil. Waterproof sandpaper and water may be used instead of pumice stone. The final sheen varies with the fineness of the powdered pumice stone, coarse powders making a dull surface and fine powders a bright sheen. For very smooth surfaces with high polish the final rubbing is done with rottenstone and oil. Varnish and lacquer can be made to dry dull in the first place, but the result is not quite the same as that produced by rubbing.

FINISHING EXTERIOR DOUGLAS-FIR PLYWOOD

Douglas-fir plywood for exterior use nearly always has a flat-grain surface with broad summerwood (dark color) bands. A wood surface of this kind does not hold exterior coatings so well as a vertical grain surface, which has narrow summerwood bands. In addition, weathering tends to check plywood much more than lumber of the sames pecies. This checking often extends through the coating to detract from its appearance and durability. The checking, however, does not indicate serious deterioration of the plywood or a tendency for it to delaminate.

Finishing Suggestions

The following four finishes for exterior Douglas-fir plywood are listed in the order of most to least preferred:

1. Heavily pigmented, oil-base stain.
2. Aluminum paint primer with oil-base paint topcoats.
3. Sanded oil-base paint.
4. Emulsion paint.

Each finish is discussed briefly in the following paragraphs.

Stain

Heavily pigmented, oil-base stains are usually called shingle stains or heavy-bodied stains. They come in dark browns, reds, greens, and yellows. They penetrate and color wood, obscuring its grain but leaving little or no surface film. They are preferred for finishing plywood because they are durable, have no tendency to peel, and will make the surface checks inconspicuous. Other stains for exterior wood, often called natural finishes or redwood stains, are also available. They have less pigment in them and thus will not be as durable and will not do as well in hiding the "wild grain" of plywood that some consider, from the appearance standpoint, as undesirable on exterior surfaces.

Aluminum Primer and Oil Paint Topcoats

If a house paint with a smooth rather than a textured appearsance is preferred for your Douglas-fir plywood, the bare wood should be primed with an aluminum paint for wood, sometimes called aluminum house paint. Do not use an aluminum paint for metal and masonry or one that is described loosely as an all-purpose paint. Apply two coats of the house paint over the aluminum primer.

Sanded Oil-Base Paints

If a paint finish is preferred, it has been found that the old-fashioned sanded paint finish is durable on exterior plywood. The system consists of one priming coat of house paint primer, which was allowed to dry, then a second coat of house paint, on which ordinary builders' sand is sprinkled generously while the paint is wet, followed finally by a third coat of house paint after the sanded coat dried.

The sanded paint presents the appearance of stucco or painted cement rather than of smooth, painted wood. The finish is more expensive than ordinary coatings of house paint, both because of the labor of sanding and because the final coat of paint takes a gallon for about 150 rather than 600 to 700 square feet of surface. The long life and good appearance, however, may justify the extra cost.

Emulsion Paints

Emulsion (water-base) paints have become quite popular in recent years and are reported to be promising when applied on Douglas-fir plywood. It is suggested that the specific recommendations of the paint manufacturer be followed in using an emulsion paint on Douglas-fir plywood. An emulsion system would be far easier to apply than the sanded paint system and is probably worthy of consideration and further investigation.

APPLYING A POYLURETHANE RESIN FINISH TO WOOD STABILIZED WITH A POLYETHYLENE GLYCOL TREATMENT

The only finish known that will dry properly on the waxy surface of wood that has been treated with polyethylene glycol to give it stability is polyurethane resin (single component) finish. The polyethylene glycol treatment has a considerable effect on the manner of surface preparation and finishing procedure; it must be done carefully and correctly. The following steps are recommended for a successful finish job.

1. Initial Sanding

Sand initially with very coarse sandpaper, stroking with the grain. Fine or medium papers will clog quickly and thus cannot be used for this first sanding.

2. Bleaching of Dark Areas

Owing to the nature of the polyethylene glycol treating process, there may be an accumulation of about 1/16-inch thickness of dark material near the surface of the wood. These materials are concentrations of pigments, minerals, and extractives, and may be removed by brushing on a solution of 4 heaping tablespoons of oxalic acid crystals in a cup of hot water. Extreme care should be used in handling oxalic acid, as it is a poison. After about an hour of drying, remove and neutralize the excess acid by sponging with a cloth dampened with a dilute solution of household ammonia. Allow 24 hours of drying time before proceeding with the finish sanding.

3. Finish Sanding

Using wet-or-dry sandpaper (4/0) and hot water for lubricant, sand out all rough spots and scratches. Allow the wood to dry thoroughly before proceeding with step 4.

4. Application of Sealing Coat

Stir polyurethane resin finish thoroughly and then pour into clean container, mixing in an equal volume of turpentine or mineral spirits. Apply to wood. Allow 24 hours for drying; then sand lightly with 6/0 paper.

5. Application of Toner-Filler

When toner-fillers are to be used, shake thoroughly and apply liberally with a clean brush, stroking with the grain. After ½ hour of drying or when the solvent has evaporated, work the filler into the pores by rubbing across the grain with a soft cloth or the palm of your hand. Allow to dry at least 1 day in a warm, well-ventilated room. When thoroughly dry, sand lightly with 6/0 paper.

6. Final Finish Coats

Apply the first finish coat of polyurethane resin full strength or diluted only slightly. Allow to dry, sand lightly with 6/0 paper, and then rub with 3/0 steel wool, being extremely careful not to cut through the finish. Then apply the final coat or coats. Four or five finish coats will result in a really professional-looking job. Sand lightly between each coat with 6/0 paper and follow this with light rubbing with 3/0 steel wool. After final coat has dried thoroughly, polish with fine pumice and an oil lubricant. Further protection may be achieved by applying furniture polish, wax, oil, or whatever you desire.

General Comments

The stabilizing chemical, polyethylene glycol will quickly absorb water vapor from the air during hot, humid weather. The resulting film of moisture that forms on the wood surface can prevent the sealer, filler, or finish coats from setting firmly or adhering properly. For this reason, polyethylene glycol treated wood should not be finished during hot and humid weather unless done in an air-conditioned room. If finish drying difficulties are encountered, dry the wood before continuing the finishing process.

Polyurethane resin finish will normally set within an hour or so in a warm, dry atmosphere. If desired, the drying time can be reduced by adding a little (a few drops) additional hardener (6 percent cobalt naphthenate) to the finish just prior to application. If added earlier, the supply of finish will solidify in the container.

Checkering or like processes should be completed prior to application of finish coats due to the hardness of the polyurethane resin finish.

EFFECTIVENESS OF MOISTURE-EXCLUDING COATINGS SUITABLE FOR INTERIOR USE

Shrinking and swelling and stresses in wood that cause warping, checking, and weathering are brought about by changes in the moisture content. Such changes occur whenever wood is exposed to varying atmospheric conditions. Effective protection against fluctuating atmospheric conditions is furnished by coatings of various moisture-retardant finishes provided that the coating is applied to all surfaces of wood through which moisture might gain access. No coating is entirely moisture-proof, however, and there is as yet no way of keeping moisture out of wood that is exposed to dampness constantly or for prolonged periods.

The comparative effectiveness of various common coatings in protecting wood at 11-percent moisture content against absorption of moisture during 2 weeks' exposure to nearly saturated air is given in the following tabulation in which perfect protection would be represented by 100-percent effectiveness; complete lack of protection, as with uncoated wood, by zero.

Description:	Percent effectiveness
3 coats of aluminum powder in gloss oil (quick drying) or in varnish	92
3 coats of aluminum powder in shellac	92
Heavy coating of paraffin	91
3 coats of rubbing varnish	89
3 coats of shellac	87
3 coats of enamel (cellulose-lacquer vehicle)	76
3 coats of cellulose lacquer	73
3 coats of gloss oil bronzing liquid	12
3 coats of furniture wax	8

UNEVEN COATINGS ON WOOD CAUSE WARPING

Coatings of equal moisture resistance should be applied to all surfaces of wood products if they are to be kept entirely free from warp under changing atmospheric conditions. Tests have shown that no coating entirely prevents wood from picking up or giving off moisture and, consequently, from swelling and shrinking under the influence of varying atmospheric conditions. Varnish, shellac, and other moisture-resistant finishes merely decrease the rate at which the moisture changes in wood occur. Ordinarily the higher the grade and the more coats applied, the slower will be the moisture changes.

Unequal coatings on opposite surfaces of a wooden article cause unequal rates of change in moisture content and hence unequal shrinkage on the two sides of the piece. The result is that the wood tends to cup or twist out of shape.

Inexpensive coatings can be applied to the backs of furniture or millwork which will be practically equal in moisture resistance to the face surface coatings. These coatings for backs can usually be applied in one or two coats, depending on the moisture resistance required.

CHEMICAL TREATMENT FOR CONTROL OF SHRINKAGE AND SWELLING OF WOOD

A chemical treatment that imparts a high degree of dimensional stability to wood has been developed by the Forest Products Laboratory. The chemical used is polyethylene glycol-1000. The "1000" refers to the average molecular weight of this compound. It is a first cousin of permanent-type antifreeze, and is a member of a whole family of polyethylene glycols having varying molecular weights, solubilities, freezing and boiling points, and other properties. Polyethylene glycol-1000 is a white waxlike chemical that resembles paraffin. It dissolves readily in warm water, is nontoxic, noncorrosive, melts at 104° F., and has a very high (580° F.) fire point.

There are two different applications for which this treatment is being considered: (1) to dimensionally stabilize wood, and (2) to prevent or reduce degradation (checking) of the wood during drying.

Dimensional stabilization requires a high degree of penetration of polyethylene glycol into the wood. To obtain high dimensional stability, a penetration of the chemical throughout the wood is required leading to a uniform uptake of 25 to 30 percent of chemical based on the weight of the dry wood. The time necessary for this uptake depends on the thickness of the wood and may require weeks. It is fully effective only on green wood or wood that has been thoroughly water soaked.

Reduction of checking during drying can be obtained by a much less drastic treatment of the wood than that required for dimensional stabilization purposes. Here the polyethylene glycol is used as a chemical seasoning agent and only impregnation of the outer surface is required. This method of treatment has been used to advantage to reduce checking during drying of small wood blanks or turnings.

An application in which the treatment of wood with polyethylene glycol has so far proven to be advantageous is in the manufacture of green-wood carvings, turnings, and various craft items in which a relatively light treatment is effective in reducing face checking during drying (fig. 34). In this application the objective is simply to get enough polyethylene glycol into the outer surface to reduce degradation during drying rather than to obtain dimensional stability in which a high degree of absorption of chemical throughout the wood is required.

Another example of the use of polyethylene glycol is in the treatment of precarved green gunstock blanks (fig. 35). When semi-inletted stocks shaped from green wood are heavily treated with polyethylene glycol-1000 they can be safely dried from the dripping wet condition to 6 percent moisture condition in 20 days. Moreover, the critical areas around the action and barrel groove are highly dimensionally stable. In these areas the wood is relatively thin and good penetration is obtained. To obtain a high level of dimensional stability, it is necessary to soak the green stocks in the chemical for relatively long periods — up to 6 weeks. Treating time, however, can be reduced by increasing the temperature of the treating solution.

For best results, the chemical must be applied to the green wood fresh from the saw. Treatment of precarved stocks or stock blanks at this stage practically eliminates splits, checks, internal honeycomb, and other degrade during seasoning, and permits accelerated drying according to a kiln schedule far more drastic than that normally recommended for walnut gunstock blanks. Or, the treated wood can be air dried over a longer period with equally good results. Studies indicate that even highly figured woods like Oregon myrtle, curly bird's-eye maple, and some wild-grain tropical species — all known to be bad actors from the standpoint of tendency to split, check, and warp during drying — can be seasoned without significant degrade with this process.

It is believed that chemically stabilized stocks will outperform any substitute material thus far developed and at the same time retain the natural warmth, beauty, durability, and other desirable properties of the fine hardwoods long prized by American sportsmen.

Practically all wooden art carvings from tropical countries— southeast Asia, Equatorial Africa, Latin America, and other areas of high humidity — are made of poorly seasoned wood that is only partially dry. As a consequence, the majority of such carvings check or split badly when they are brought into the United

Figure 34. — Green-wood carvings the size and shape of this Irish setter are exceedingly difficult to dry defect-free without treatment with polyethylene glycol, which is 100 percent effective in preventing seasoning degrade.

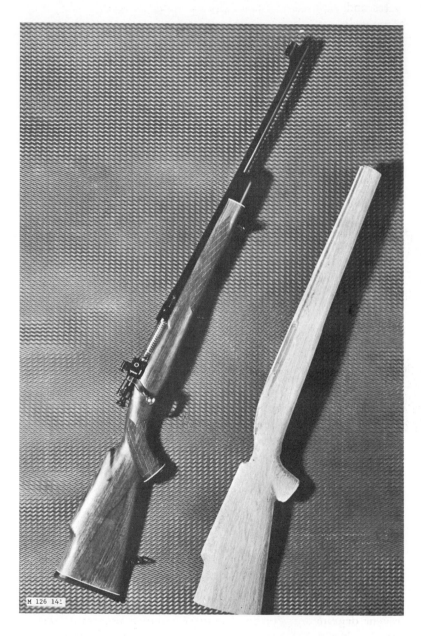

Figure 35. — *Precarved (from green wood), chemically treated, kiln-dried walnut stocks, one finished and fitted to sporterized Springfield M1903A3 and the other as it appeared when taken from the kiln.*

States and exposed to our relatively low humidities. Many are completely ruined after only 1 or 2 weeks in the arid environment of our heated stores, offices, and homes.

Timely treatment with polyethylene glycol-1000 will effectively prevent the development of checks and splits in carvings made of partially dry wood, regardless of how rapidly or completely they are dried following stabilization. The procedure is essentially the same as that for seasoning green-wood carvings— that is, carvings made from fresh-cut absolutely green wood. The chief difference is that the partially dry carvings must be soaked in water previous to immersion in the stabilizing chemical (figs. 36 and 37).

Treating wood with polyethylene glycol-1000 promises to open new horizons in bowl turning by hobbyists and others.

The maximum depth of solid wooden bowls made from dry wood is normally limited to three or four inches, or the thickness possible or practical to dry wood without defect. On the other hand, bowls made from green or only partially dry wood— a common practice — frequently split, check, or warp as the wood dries. Even when thoroughly dry wood is used, the turnings may warp, split, or change dimension with changes in atmospheric moisture conditions. That is why so many of the wooden bowls you see are slightly elliptical rather than round.

The procedure of using polyethylene glycol-1000 is simple. The wood is turned while green, and the rough turnings are put immediately in a 30 percent (by weight) solution of polyethylene glycol-1000 and soaked for about 3 weeks at a room temperature of 70° to 75° F. The water-soluble, wax-like chemical diffuses readily into the green wood, and the bulking action of the large molecules curbs shrinkage and prevents checking, splitting, and warping. The treated bowls can be air dried to a moisture content of 6 or 7 percent and then turned and finished to the desired size. Or they can be dried under more drastic conditions without degrade. Treated bowls, once dry and finished, will resist further dimensional changes with variations in atmospheric moisture conditions (fig. 38).

Other applications are the use of polyethylene glycol to prevent degradation during drying of wooden objects of scientific and historic interest that have been buried or submerged

*Figure 36.—Untreated carving split in two after several months of drying
in a heated home.*

Figure 37. — Carving was dried to flawless perfection following treatment with polyethylene glycol.

Figure 38.—Polyethylene glycol-1000 treated bowls that have been turned to final dimensions, sanded, finished, and polished.

in water for centuries, and the use of polyethylene glycol as a chemical seasoning agent for green shoe-last blanks.

According to the manufacturers, the polyethylene glycols have relatively low order of toxicity. Polyethylene glycol therefore has little effect as a toxic material in preventing decay. This chemical reduces decay only when the wood is treated to such a high retention of chemical that the moisture adsorption by the wood substance is reduced to a level below that which will support decay. Stated differently, the chemical imparts decay resistance only when it imparts high dimensional stability.

Since polyethylene glycol is water soluble, it is readily leached out of the wood when exposed to liquid water. Leaching of the chemical can be greatly reduced by a good surface coating. Polyurethane resin-base varnish has proven satisfactory as a surface finish when applied to the rather wax-like surface of the treated wood. Polyethylene glycol treatment causes many other finishes to dry more slowly or to adhere poorly to the treated wood.

Resorcinol glues have been used successfully in the gluing of polyethylene glycol treated gunstock blanks.

Many of the large chemical companies in this country and in Europe produce polyethylene glycol.

It is obviously impossible to make blanket recommendations regarding the use of polyethylene glycol. For best results it is necessary to develop a treatment schedule specifically tailored for a particular product, wood species, and use requirement.

GLUING OF WOOD

The use of glue in the fabrication of wood products makes possible the production of articles of unusual form, dimensions, and properties. It also brings about more complete utilization of wood through the use of lower grades and small sizes of material. Nearly every article of glued-wood construction represents an economy in the use of timber resources.

Modern glues, processes, and techniques vary as widely as the products made, and developments have been many in recent years. In general, however, it remains true that the quality of a glued joint depends upon (1) the kind of wood and its preparation for use, (2) the kind and quality of the glue and its preparation for use, (3) the details of the gluing process, (4) the types of joints, and (5) the conditioning of the joints. Depending on the glue used, service conditions also affect the performance of the joint to a greater or lesser extent.

GLUING PROPERTIES OF DIFFERENT WOODS

Table 4 gives the gluing properties of the most important woods that are glued. The classification is based on the average strength of side-grain joints of approximately average density wood of each species, when glued with animal, casein, starch, urea resin, and resorcinol resin glues. A species is considered to be glued satisfactorily when the strength of the joint obtained is approximately equal to the strength of the wood.

In addition to the major woodworking glues listed in table 5, glues made from a base of blood albumin have had very limited use in the United States but are more commonly used in Europe in the production of plywood. They are mixed at the time of use and are applied at room temperatures, but most of them require hot pressing. They are highly water resistant but not so durable as some of the synthetic resin glues. Defibrinated blood is sometimes used as a filler or extender for phenol resin glues.

Many brands of glues made from fish, animal, or vegetable derivatives are sold in liquid form, ready for application. Their principal use in woodworking is for small jobs and repair work. They are variable in quality and low in water resistance and durability under damp conditions. The better brands are moderate in dry strength and set fairly quickly. They are applied cold, usually by brush, and are pressed cold. They stain wood only slightly, if at all.

The ease or difficulty with which satisfactory joints are made is dependent on the density of the wood, the structure of the wood, the presence of chemical substances in the wood, and the kind of glue. In general, heavy woods are more difficult to glue than lightweight woods, hardwoods more difficult than softwoods, and heartwood more difficult than sapwood. A few woods, notably basswood, hickory, the gums, and the heartwood of baldcypress and of eastern red cedar vary considerably in their gluing characteristics with the different adhesives.

Table 4. – *Classification of various hardwood and softwood species according to gluing properties*

HARDWOODS

Group 1 (Glue very easily with different glues under wide range of gluing conditions)	Group 2 (Glue well with different glues under a moderately wide range of gluing conditions)	Group 3 (Glue satisfactorily under well-controlled gluing conditions)	Group 4 (Require very close control of gluing conditions, or special treatment to obtain best results)
Aspen	Alder, red	Ash, white[2]	Beech, American
Chestnut, American	Basswood[1]	Cherry, black[1, 2]	Birch, sweet and yellow[2]
Cottonwood	Butternut[1, 2]	Dogwood[2]	Hickory[2]
Willow, black	Elm:	Maple, soft[1, 2]	Maple, hard
Yellow-poplar	American[2]	Oak:	Osage-orange
	Rock[1, 2]	Red[2]	Persimmon
	Hackberry	White	
	Magnolia[1, 2]	Pecan	
	Mahogany[2]	Sycamore[1, 2]	
	Sweetgum[1]	Tupelo:	
		Black[1]	
		Water[1, 2]	
		Walnut, black	

SOFTWOODS

Baldcypress	Cedar, eastern red[2]	Cedar, Alaska[2]	
Cedar, westernred[3]	Douglas-fir		
Fir, white	Hemlock, western[3]		
Larch, western	Pine:		
Redwood	Eastern white[3]		
Spruce, Sitka	Southern yellow[1]		
	Ponderosa		

[1] Species is more subject to starved joints, particularly with animal glue, than the classification would otherwise indicate.
[2] Glued more easily with resin glues than with nonresin glues.
[3] Glued more easily with nonresin glues than with resin glues.

Glues Used in Woodworking

Table 5 describes briefly the characteristics, preparation, and uses of the types of glue most commonly used to make joints in wood.

Animal glues have long been used extensively in woodworking; starch glues came into general use, especially for veneering, early in this century; casein glue and vegetable protein glues, of which soybean is the most important, gained commercial importance during and immediately following World War I for gluing lumber and veneer into products that required moderate water resistance. Synthetic resin glues were developed during World War II, but now surpass many of the older glues in importance as woodworking glues. Phenol resin glues are widely used to produce plywood for severe service conditions. Urea resin glues are used extensively in producing plywood for furniture and interior paneling. Resorcinol and phenol-resorcinol resin glues are useful for gluing lumber into products that will withstand exposure to the weather. Polyvinyl resin emulsion glues are used in assembly joints of furniture.

Broadly, synthetic resin glues are of two types — thermosetting and thermoplastic. Thermosetting resins, once cured, are not softened by heat. Thermoplastic resins will soften when reheated.

There are various other adhesive substances including cellulose cements, rubber cements, sodium silicates, mucilages, pastes, asphalts, gums, and shellac, some of which are used to a limited extent for gluing wood; but of insufficient importance to justify detailed discussion.

The purposes for which glues are used in woodworking may be grouped broadly as the gluing of veneer and the gluing of joints in thick stock. Liquid glues are used mainly for joints of small area which are subjected to low stress, such as those in repair work and in small jobs of hand gluing. Animal glue finds a wide variety of uses both in small jobs and in larger-scale production, particularly for joints in thick stock. Casein glues, starch glues, vegetable-protein glues, and synthetic resin glues are used mainly in larger-scale production, such as plywood and door manufacturing operations. Casein glues are also marketed in packages for the smaller user. Some of the synthetic

Table 5. — *Characteristics, preparation, and uses of the most commonly used woodworking glues*

Class	Form and testing	Properties	Preparation and application	Uses
Animal	Many grades sold in dry form; liquid glues available; quality determined by tests on solutions of the glue.	High dry strength; low resistance to moisture and damp conditions; stain wood very slightly, if at all.	Dry form mixed with water, soaked, and melted; solution kept warm during application; liquid forms applied as received; both pressed at room temperatures.	Used extensively in furniture assembly joints, cabinetmaking, and millwork.
Casein and vegetable protein	Several brands sold in dry powder form; may also be prepared from raw materials by user; quality determined by tests on glue and by tests on wood joints.	High to low dry strength; moderate to low water resistance and moderately durable under damp conditions; pronounced dulling effect on tools; stain some woods badly.	Mixed with cold water, applied and pressed cold.	Used for gluing lumber and veneer for purposes requiring moderate moisture resistance.
Starch	Different grades sold in dry form; also available in liquid form ready to use; quality determined chiefly by tests on wood joints.	High in dry strength; low resistance to moisture and damp conditions; stain some woods moderately.	Dry forms mixed with water, usually with addition of caustic soda, and heated; applied cold; liquid form applied as received; both pressed cold.	Used primarily in gluing veneer.
Urea resin	Several brands sold as dry powder, others as liquids; may be blended with melamine or other resins; quality determined by tests on glue and by tests on wood joints.	High in both wet and dry strength; moderately durable under damp conditions; moderate to low resistance to temperatures in excess of 150° F.; white or tan in color; stain wood very slightly if at all.	Dry form mixed with water, hardeners, fillers, and extenders may be added by user to either dry or liquid form; applied at room temperatures, some formulas cure at room temperatures, others require hot pressing at about 250° F.	Used extensively in gluing veneer for furniture and other interior uses and to some extent in gluing lumber and assembly joints.

Table 5. — *Characteristics, preparation, and uses of the most commonly used woodworking glues (contd.)*

Melamine resin	Comparatively few brands available; usually marketed as a powder with or without catalyst; quality determined by tests on glue and by tests on wood joints.	High in both wet and dry strength; very resistant to moisture and damp conditions; stain wood very slightly, if at all; white to tan in color.	Mixed with water and applied at room temperatures; heat required to cure (250° to 350° F.)	Used to a limited extent in bag molding and in gluing lumber and veneer for purposes requiring colorless and highly resistant glue lines.
Phenol resin	Several brands available, some dry powders, others as liquids, and one as dry film; quality determined by tests on glue and by tests on wood joints.	High in both wet and dry strength; very resistant to moisture and damp conditions, more resistant than wood to high temperatures; stain wood very slightly; dark red in color.	Film form used as received; powder form mixed with solvent, often alcohol and water, at room temperature; hardeners and fillers often added by users; most common types require hot pressing at about 300° F.	Used primarily for production of highly resistant plywood.
Resorcinol resin	Several brands available in liquid form; catalyst supplied separately; some brands are combinations of phenol and resorcinol resins; relatively high priced; quality determined by tests on glue and by tests on wood joints.	High in both wet and dry strength; very resistant to moisture and damp conditions; more resistant than wood to high temperatures; stain wood very slightly; dark red in color.	Mixed with catalyst and applied at room temperatures; resorcinol glues cure at room temperatures; some resorcinol-phenol blends cure best under moderate heat (100° to 200° F.).	Used primarily for gluing lumber or assembly joints that must withstand severe service conditions.
Polyvinyl emulsion resin	Several brands are available, varying to some extent in properties; marketed in liquid form ready to use; quality determined largely by tests on glue joints.	Generally high in dry strength; low resistance to moisture and elevated temperatures; joints tend to yield under continued stress; white in color; stain wood little if at all.	Marketed as a liquid ready to use; applied and pressed at room temperatures.	Used in assembly joints in furniture, cabinetmaking, and millwork.

resin glues require the use of presses equipped with heated platens, others are available ready-mixed in small quantities.

Household or small-package glues, such as used by the home woodworker, frequently include special formulations developed primarily for occasional use for a much wider variation of applications than that required for large scale industrial adhesives. Small-package glues must have good storage stability, or shelf life, before use since they are applied essentially by hand in small operations, they must be usable with simple clamping equipment and under rather imperfectly controlled bonding conditions.

STRENGTH OF COMMERCIAL LIQUID GLUES

Most of the commercial liquid glues are manufactured from the skins, heads, and swimming bladders of fish. Others are made by special treatment of the glue extracted from the hides, skins and bones of cattle; some for special uses are prepared from starch, natural gums, or casein.

At the Forest Products Laboratory tests have been made on a number of liquid glues, which were found to differ very widely in strength. Some of them were so weak as to be entirely unsuitable for woodworking purposes, whereas others compare favorably in strength with the "hot" glues. The glues tested varied from one which exerted a binding force of less than 50 pounds per square inch to one with an adhesive strength 60 times as great, giving a shearing strength of more than 3,000 pounds per square inch.

In addition to uniformly high adhesive strength, certain other characteristics are desired in a liquid glue. The glue in joints should not soften materially on damp days. When spread upon wood surfaces, it should "set" and dry rapidly. In its container, it should remain fluid and workable at all ordinary temperatures. It should not be unusually susceptible to the action of molds, bacteria, or high temperatures.

The strength of liquid glue, like that of "hot" glue, depends largely upon its "body" or thickness, or, strictly speaking, upon its viscosity. As a general rule the more viscous glues produce the stronger joints particularly in repair work where the interval between spreading and pressing is short.

TENDENCY OF WOODS TO BE STAINED
BY STRONGLY ALKALINE GLUE

Marked	*Slight*	*Very slight or none*
Baldcypress	Basswood	Ash
Beech	Gum, tupelo	Cottonwood
Birch	Pine, northern	Elm, soft
Cherry, black	white	Pine, ponderosa
Douglas-fir	Spruce, Sitka	Pine, southern
Mahogany	Sycamore	yellow
Maple		Yellow-poplar
Oak, red		
Oak, white		
Redwood		
Sweetgum		
Walnut, black		

In gluing thin pieces of wood the tendency of the different woods to be stained by the glue is often a matter of importance. The tendency of various woods to stain when glued with a strongly alkaline glue is given in the foregoing classification. Most discoloration of the wood when glued is the result of a reaction between the free alkali of the glue and the materials in the wood. The shade varies for different woods. For example, in oak the discoloration is brown; in mahogany, dark red; and in redwood, almost black. The different kinds of glues vary in their tendency to stain. (See table 5.) Synthetic resin glues normally contain no free alkali; nevertheless the darker-colored resins may penetrate porous woods to such an extent as to discolor thin veneers. Animal and liquid glues do not normally produce any objectionable discoloration.

Staining may be reduced by drying the wood to a low moisture content before it is glued and then drying the glued stock as soon as possible after the glue is applied. Surface stains may be removed by bleaching. Sponging the stained surface with an oxalic-acid solution, prepared by dissolving 1 ounce of oxalic-acid crystals in about 12 ounces of water, will ordinarily remove glue discoloration. A more effective way is to moisten the wood first with a sodium-sulphite solution (1 ounce sodium sulphite to 12 ounces water) followed by the application of oxalic acid. The acid must be thoroughly removed from the wood afterwards or it may affect the finish. The oxalic acid is poisonous and should be handled with care.

TREATING THE WOOD BEFORE GLUING

Treating certain woods with a chemical before gluing improves the joint strength. A 10 percent solution of caustic soda is quite effective. The wood surfaces to be joined are brushed with the caustic soda solution; after about 10 minutes they are wiped with a cloth to remove any excess solution or dissolved material and allowed to dry before being glued. This treatment decidedly improves the joint strength of the hard maple, yellow birch, white oak, red oak, red gum (both heartwood and sapwood), black cherry, and basswood. Osage-orange treated with the caustic solution and then glued with a casein glue gave satisfactory joints.

Although chemical treatments of surfaces before gluing result in better joints with certain woods that require great care in gluing, such treatments are time consuming and therefore add to the expense of gluing. Ordinarily, good glued joints can be secured by properly regulating the gluing practice so that the chemical treatment of the wood is unnecessary.

DRYING AND MOISTURE CONDITIONING WOOD FOR GLUING

The moisture content of wood at the time of gluing has much to do with the final strength of joints, development of checks in the wood, and warping of the glued members. Satisfactory adhesion of glue to wood is obtained at any moisture content of the wood up to 15 percent and even higher with water-resistant glues. Large changes in the moisture content of the wood after gluing, however, develop stresses that may seriously weaken both the wood and the joints.

The most satisfactory moisture content of wood at the time of gluing is that which, when increased by the moisture of the glue, approximately equals the average moisture content that the glued member will have in service. In gluing thick pieces this relation can be attained, but in gluing veneer or other thin pieces the moisture added by the glue frequently exceeds the moisture content of the wood in service. Under the latter conditions the wood cannot be dried enough before gluing to avoid redrying of the glued products afterward. The amount of moisture added to wood in gluing varies from less than 1 percent in lumber to 45 percent or more in thin plywood. The thickness of the wood, the number of plies, the density of the wood, the glue mixture, and the quantity of glue spread all affect the increase in moisture content of the wood.

In general practice adjustments cannot be made for all these widely varying factors, and it is seldom that wood need be dried to a moisture content below 5 percent or higher than 12 percent. Lumber with a moisture content of 5 to 6 percent is satisfactory for gluing into furniture and similar uses. Lumber for outside use should generally contain 10 to 12 percent of moisture before gluing. Experience has shown that a moisture content of 5 percent in veneer at the time of gluing is satisfactory for even thin plywood and veneer in furniture and similar products.

Lumber that has been dried to the approximate average moisture content desired for gluing may still show differences between various boards and between the center and the outside of individual pieces. Large differences in the moisture content of the pieces at the time of gluing result eventually in considerable stress on glue joints and tend to produce warping of the product. Hence, it is desirable for many purposes to condition wood to a relatively uniform moisture content after drying and before gluing. Small variations of 1 percent or less between boards of the same species and size may be disregarded since they may occur even after a long conditioning period. Lumber that is to be glued should also be free from drying defects.

MACHINING LUMBER FOR GLUING

Wood surfaces that are to be glued should be smooth and true. Machining should preferably be done just before gluing so that the surfaces do not become distorted from subsequent moisture changes. In panel constructions the thickness of each lamination or ply should be uniform, that is, it should not be thinner in one part than in another. A small variation in thick-

ness in each piece may cause a total difference of serious proportions when a number of similar pieces are piled in the same
order as they come from the surfacer. Machine marks, chipped
or loosened grain, and other surface irregularities are objectionable.

Surfaces made by a saw are usually rougher than those
made by planers, jointers, and other machines equipped with
cutter heads, but recent perfection of saws for this purpose
has made it possible to glue sawed joints more extensively and
thereby to effect a saving of labor and material. In cabinet work
and other constructions where joints are exposed to view, the
sawed joint is not always satisfactory because it is usually more
conspicuous than the planed joint.

Intentional roughening of wood surfaces by tooth planing,
scratching, or sanding with coarse sandpaper is practiced by
some operators in the belief that it affords better surfaces for
gluing. However, tests of joints made under good gluing practice
show no benefit from roughening the surfaces.

Preparing Veneer for Gluing

Veneer for gluing is cut by sawing, slicing, or rotary processes. Sawed veneer is produced in long narrow strips usually
from flitches selected for figure and grain. It is equally firm
and strong on both sides of the sheet and either side may be
glued or exposed to view with similar results.

Sliced veneer is also cut in the form of long strips by moving
a flitch or block against a heavy knife. The veneer is forced
abruptly away from the flitch by the knife, thus causing fine
checks or breaks on the knife side. The checked side is called
the open or loose side, and the other side is called the closed
or tight side. The open side is likely to show defects in finishing and therefore should be the glue side whenever possible.
For matching face stock where the open side of part of the
sheets must be the finish side, the veneer must be well cut.

Most rotary-cut veneer is produced in large sheets by revolv-
ing a log against a knife, flat-grain veneer being peeled off in a
continuous sheet. The half-round process, a modification of
straight rotary cutting is used to produce highly figured veneer
from stumps, burls, and other irregular parts of logs. This

process consists of placing a part of a log, stump, or burl off center in a lathe and rotary cutting it into small sheets of veneer. All rotary-cut veneer has an open and a closed side. As with sliced veneer, the checked or open side should be the glue side whenever possible.

Veneer is not usually resurfaced before it is glued, and the care with which it is cut is therefore of prime importance. Provided the veneer is well cut there is no appreciable difference in the strength and other properties, except appearance, of the plywood made from veneer produced by any of the three processes. The characteristics important in selecting veneer to be glued are (1) uniformity of thickness in the same piece, (2) smoothness and flatness, (3) freedom from large checks or other defects, and (4) straightness of grain and absence of decay.

Proper Gluing Conditions

A strong joint in wood is characterized by complete contact of glue and wood surfaces over the entire joint area and a continuous film of good glue between the wood layers that is unbroken by air bubbles or by foreign particles. This result is obtained by a control of the details of the gluing operation.

Making strong glue joints with glues applied in liquid condition depends primarily upon a proper correlation between gluing pressure and glue consistency at the moment the pressure is applied. The consistency of the glue mixture after being spread on the wood is extremely variable, depending upon such factors as the kind of glue, glue-water proportion of the mixture, quantity of glue spread, moisture content of the wood, temperature of the glue, room, and wood, the time elapsing between spreading and pressing, and the extent to which the glue-coated surfaces are exposed to the air. A light pressure should be used with a thin glue, a heavy pressure with a thick glue, and corresponding variations in pressure should be made with glues of intermediate consistencies.

Joints should be retained under pressure at least until they have sufficient strength to withstand the interior stresses tending to separate the wood pieces. In cold pressing operations it is safe to assume that under favorable gluing conditions this stage will be reached in 2 to 7 hours, according to the thickness and absorptive characteristics of the wood. A pressing period beyond the minimum is advisable as a precautionary measure when operating conditions permit. In hot-pressing operations the time required varies with the temperature of the platens, the thickness and kind of material being pressed, and the kind of glue. The variation in time in actual practice is from 2 minutes to as much as 30 minutes.

Gluing with the dry forms of adhesives requires special conditions that vary somewhat with the particular adhesive and class of product.

TYPES OF GLUE JOINTS

Side-Grain Surfaces

With most kinds of wood straight, plain joints between side-grain surfaces (fig. 39) can be made substantially as strong as the wood itself in shear parallel to the grain, tension across the grain, and cleavage. Tongue-and-grove, dovetail, and other shaped joints present the theoretical advantage of larger gluing surfaces than do the straight joints, but they do not give higher strengths with most woods. Furthermore, the theoretical advantage is often lost, wholly or in part, because the shaped joints are more difficult to machine than straight plain joints so as to obtain a perfect fit of the parts. Lack of the contact may make the effective holding area actually smaller on a shaped joint than on a flat surface and thus reduce rather than increase the strength. Only under circumstances where the gluing conditions are not well controlled and the joints are weak do the larger contact surfaces of well-fitted joints improve the strength. The principal advantage of the tongue-and-groove and other shaped joints is that the parts can be more quickly aligned in the clamps or press. A shallow tongue-and-groove is usually as useful in this respect as a deeper cut and is less wasteful of wood.

End-Grain Surfaces

It is practically impossible to make end-butt joints (fig. 40) sufficiently strong or permanent to meet the requirements of ordinary service. With the most careful gluing possible not more than about 25 percent of the tensile strength of the wood parallel with the grain can be obtained in butt joints. In order to approxi-

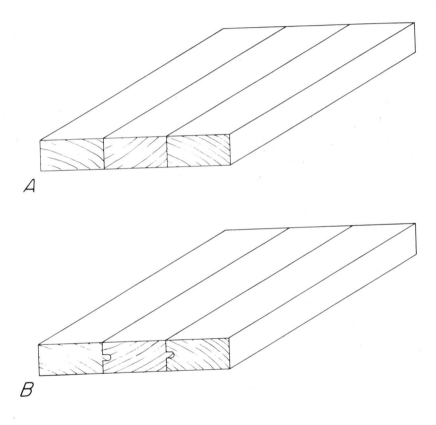

Figure 39. — Side-to-side joints: A, Plain; B, tongued-and-grooved.

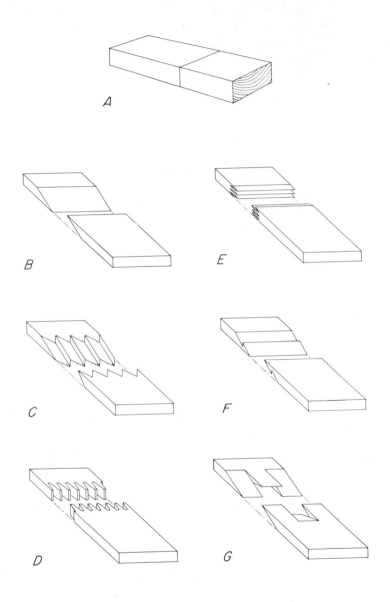

Figure 40. — End-to-end-grain joints: A, End butt; B, plain scarf; C, serrated scarf; D, finger; E, Onsrud; F, hooked scarf; G, double-slope scarf.

mate the tensile strength of various woods a scarf, serrated, or other form of joint that approaches a side-grain surface must be used. The plain scarf is perhaps the easiest to glue and entails fewer machining difficulties than the many-angle forms.

The following slopes are considered necessary to produce joints as strong in tension along the grain as the solid wood.

Species:	Slope
Birch, yellow	1 in 12
Mahogany	1 in 10
Oak, red	1 in 15
Oak, white	1 in 15
Sweetgum	1 in 8
Walnut, black	1 in 8
Yellow-poplar	1 in 15

End-to-side-grain joints (fig. 41) are also difficult to glue properly and further, are subjected in service to unusually severe stresses as a result of unequal dimensional changes in the two members of the joint with moisture-content changes. It is therefore, necessary to use irregular shapes of joints, dowels, tenons, or other devices to reinforce such a joint in order to bring side grain into contact with side grain or to secure larger gluing surfaces. All end-to-side-grain joints should be carefully protected against changes in moisture content.

Conditioning Glued Joints

In gluing lumber edge to edge the wood immediately adjacent to the joint absorbs more water from the glue and therefore swells more than the other portions of the boards. If the glued pieces are surfaced before this excess moisture is dried out or distributed, more wood is removed along the joints than at intermediate portions. Subsequently, when the moisture content becomes uniform greater shrinkage occurs at the joints than elsewhere and permanent depressions are formed. Such depressions along the glue line may be very conspicuous in a finished panel.

In gluing lumber and other thick pieces face to face, the glue moisture need not be dried out but simply allowed to distribute itself uniformly throughout the wood.

In plywood, veneered panels, and other constructions made by gluing together thin layers of wood, it is advisable to dry out a part, at least, of the moisture added in gluing in order

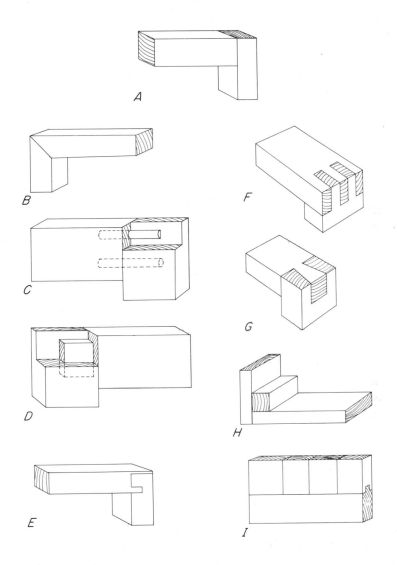

Figure 41. — End-to-side grain joints: A, Plain; B, miter; C, dowel;
D, mortise and tenon; E, dado tongue and rabbet; F, slip or lock corner;
G, dovetail; H, blocked; I, tongued-and-grooved.

to reach an average service moisture content. The drying is most advantageously done under controlled conditions and time schedules. Drying such glued products to excessively low moisture-content values materially increases warping, opening of joints, and checking.

DURABILITY OF GLUED MEMBERS

Adequate data are not available for fixing the moisture content at or below which the different glues retain their strength permanently. However, available information indicates that in well-constructed joints any of the common woodworking glues are permanently durable under conditions where wood has 15 percent moisture content or less. Joints made with nonwater-resistant glues fail quickly when exposed to damp conditions. Even the more commonly used water-resistant glue joints, which show a strength when first saturated with water of 25 to nearly 100 percent of their dry strength, fail completely when exposed without protection for a long time to free water or to extremely high relative humidity or when alternated between wet and dry conditions. Under conditions where wood retains 20 percent or more moisture there is no positive assurance of the permanence of the more common water-resistant glued joints without special treatments. The use of a glue that has natural resistance to deterioration or the addition of toxic material to the less durable glues increases the serviceability of glued products.

Low temperatures seem to have no significant effect on the strength of glue joints, but some glues have shown evidence of deterioration when exposed to temperatures of about 158° F. Joints that were well made with phenol resin, resorcinol resin, or melamine resin glues have proved more durable than the wood when exposed to water, to warmth and dampness, to alternative wetting and drying, and to temperature sufficiently high to char the wood. These glues are sufficiently durable for use in products that are exposed to the weather.

Tests have shown that joints made with urea resin glues are highly resistant to water and to wetting and drying but that they tend to weaken when subjected to temperatures of about 158° F. or higher. Casein and soybean glue joints will withstand temporary exposure to dampness or water without permanent loss in strength, but if the moisture content of the wood continuously or repeatedly exceeds about 18 percent, they will eventuaally lose strength; the rate of loss of strength may vary, however, depending upon such factors as species and construction.

Polyvinyl resin emulsion glues have moderate resistance to dampness, but low resistance to water, the tendency of the joints to yield under stress generally increases as the temperature increases. Joints made with animal glue or with starch glue are not suited to damp service conditions. If toxic materials are added to animal glues, serviceabily of the glued products in warm, damp environments is increased slightly.

Treatments of glued members that increase their durability may be grouped into two general classes: (1) Coatings that reduce the moisture content changes in the wood and glue, and (2) impregnation with preservatives or toxic materials. Effective moisture-excluding coatings are useful in reducing the magnitude of moisture-content changes in wood and glue and in lessening the weakening effect on the glue of the swelling stresses that occur during temporary periods of exposure to damp conditions. They are not effective in their protection against prolonged periods of exposure to damp conditions. Impregnation of glued members with preservatives reduces the deteriorating effects of prolonged exposure to damp conditions. The useful life of casein water-resistant plywood may be doubled or tripled by impregnations that protect both glue and wood, such as coal-tar creosote or a 10 percent solution of beta naphthol in a volatile solvent.

PLYWOOD AND OTHER CROSSBANDED PRODUCTS

Plywood is a term generally used to designate glued wood panels that are made up of 2 or more thin layers with the grain of 1 or more at an angle, usually 90°, with the others. The outside plies are called faces or face and back, the center ply or plies are called the core, and intervening plies, laid at an angle to the other plies, are called the crossbands (fig. 42). The essential features of plywood are embodied in other glued constructions with many variations of details. The core may be veneer, lumber, or various combinations of veneer and lumber, the total thickness may be less than one-sixteenth of an inch or more than 3 inches, the different plies may vary as to number, thickness, and kinds of wood, and the shape of the members

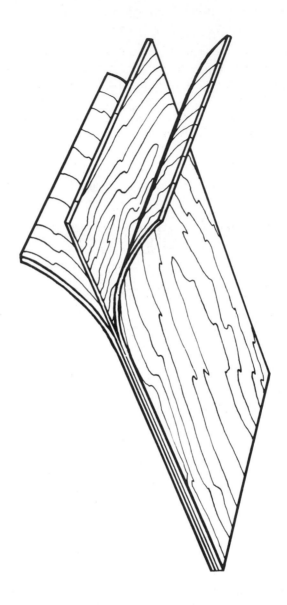

Figure 42. — How plywood is constructed. Note grain direction of adjoining plies.

may also vary. The crossbands and their arrangement largely govern the properties and uses of all such constructions.

Arrangement of Plies

The tendency of crossbanded products to warp as the result of stresses set up from shrinking and swelling with moisture-content changes is largely eliminated by balanced construction. This construction consists of arranging the plies in pairs about the core or central ply so that for each ply there is an opposite, similar, and parallel ply. Matching the plies involves a consideration of (1) thickness, (2), kind of wood with particular reference to shrinkage and density, (3) moisture content at the time of gluing, and (4) angle or relative direction of the grain.

The use of an odd number of plies permits an arrangement that gives a substantially balanced effect; that is, when 3 plies are glued together with the grain of the outer 2 plies at right angles to the grain of the center ply, the stresses are balanced and the panel tends to remain flat with moisture content changes. With 5, 7, or other uneven number of plies the forces may also be similarly balanced. If only two plies are glued together with the grain at right angles to each other, each ply tends to distort the other when moisture content changes occur, and cupping usually results. Similar results are likely when any even number of plies are used.

The use of balanced construction is highly important in thin panels that must remain flat. In thicker members some deviation from balanced construction is possible without serious consequences. For example, with lumber cores that are properly crossbanded the face and back plies may be quite dissimilar without any noticeable effect; whereas if the same face and back plies were used in thin three-ply panels, the warping might be very objectionable. In certain curved members the natural cupping tendency of an even number of plies may even be utilized advantageously.

Since the outer or face plies of a crossbanded construction are restrained on only one side, changes in moisture content induce relatively large stresses on the outer glue joints. The magniture of stresses depends upon such factors as thickness of plies, density and shrinkage of the woods involved, and the amount of the moisture-content changes. In general, one-eighth inch is about the maximum thickness of face plies that can be held securely in place when dense woods are used and large moisture changes occur.

Quality of Plies

In thin plywood the quality of all the plies affects the shape and permanence of form of the panel. The various plies should be straight grained, smoothly cut, and of sound wood, that is, of uniform growth and texture.

In thick, five-ply panels the crossbands, in particular, affect the shape and form of the panel. Imperfections in the crossbands, such as marked differences in the texture of the wood or irregularities in the surface, are easily seen in the panel through thin surface veneers. Cross grain that runs sharply through the crossband veneer from one face to the other causes the panels to cup. Cross grain that runs diagonally across the face of the crossband veneer causes a twisting of the panel unless the two crossbands are laid with the grain parallel to each other. Lack of observance of this simple precaution is accountable for much warping in crossbanded construction.

The best woods for cores of high-grade panels are those of low density and shrinkage, of slight contrast between springwood and summerwood, and of species that are glued easily. Edge-grained are better than flat-grained cores because of the lesser shrinkage in width. In softwoods with pronounced summerwood, edge-grained cores are better than flat-grained cores for the additional reason that the hard bands of summerwood are less likely to show through thin veneer. In most species a core made of all quarter-sawed or all flat-sawed material remains more uniform in thickness with moisture-content changes than one in which these two types of material are combined. This advantage is not of great practical significance, however, where the pieces of the core are narrow and the glue joints are strong.

Strength and Shrinkage of Plywood

As compared with solid wood, the chief advantages of plywood are its approach to equalization of strength properties along the length and width of the panel, greater resistance to checking and splitting, and less change in dimensions with changes in moisture content.

These advantages are obtained by alternating the direction of grain in the successive plies. Since the strength of wood across the grain is much lower than along the grain, equalization of strength properties in a plywood panel is approached through an increase in strength in one direction accompanied by a decrease in strength in the other direction. Thus, a piece of plywood acting as a simple beam with the direction of the grain in the face plies parallel to the direction of span is not so strong as a piece of ordinary wood with its grain parallel to the direction of span. On the other hand, plywood has much greater bending strength across the grain of the face plies than solid wood has across the grain.

The greater the number of plies for a given thickness, the more nearly equal are the strength properties along and across the panel and the greater the resistance to splitting. Furthermore, the shrinkage of plywood with five or more plies is somewhat less than that of three-ply material and more nearly equal in directions parallel and perpendicular to the face grain.

Splitting Resistance

Plywood permits fastening with nails or screws close to the edges because it offers much greater resistance to splitting than ordinary wood. Also, because of the equalization of strength properties along and across a sheet and the resistance to splitting resulting from the crossbanded construction, plywood panels covering relative large areas are less liable to damage from concentrated or impact loads than similar panels made of ordinary lumber.

In removing nails from plywood some care must be used to pull them straight out or nearly so, because splintering of the outside ply may result if the nails are pulled or pried out at an angle.

Shrinkage of Plywood

The shrinkage of plywood varies with the kinds of woods, the ratios of ply thicknesses, the number of plies, and the combination of woods. The average shrinkage values obtained at the Forest Products Laboratory in drying, from a soaked to an oven-dry condition, three-ply panels having all plies in any one panel of the same thickness and species was about 0.45 percent parallel to the face grain and 0.67 percent perpendicular to the face grain, with ranges of from 0.2 to 1 percent and 0.3 to 1.2 percent, respectively. The panels tested ranged in thickness from one-tenth-to one-half-inch. The shrinkage parallel and perpendicular to the face grain of plywood made of 5 or more plies is more nearly equal than that made of 3 plies.

Plywood Sizes

The unit of measurement commonly used in purchasing plywood is the square foot, surface measure, and prices may be quoted on a unit of 1,000 square feet of specified thickness, grade, and type.

There is considerable variation in panel sizes of commercially available plywood, the greatest difference being between softwood and hardwood plywood.

The most common sheet size in softwood is 4 feet by 8 feet. About 75 percent of all Douglas-fir plywood is produced in this size, and consequently is usually easiest to get. Other standard widths of Douglas-fir plywood are 36 and 60 inches. In several grades, standard lengths range from 5 to 12 feet in multiples of 1 foot. With a few exceptions, standard thicknesses range from one-fourth to three-fourths inch. Sheathing starts at five-sixteenths inch, and concrete form comes only as five-eights and three-fourths inch thick. A few sizes and grades of exterior plywood are available in thicknesses of seven-eights and 1 inch. About one-third of the Douglas-fir plywood production is in one-fourth inch and possibly two-thirds included in the range five-eighths inch and thinner. Three-ply is standard up to three-eighths inch thick, five-ply up to three-fourths inch, and seven-ply beyond. Overlaid Douglas-fir plywood is available in the 48-inch width and the 8-foot length.

Standard sizes of western softwood plywood range from 3 to 5 feet in width in multiples of 1 foot, and from 5 to 12 feet in length in multiples of 1 foot. Thicknesses range from one-fourth to three-fourths inch in three- and five-ply construction.

Ponderosa pine, sugar pine, and Idaho white pine plywood are made in about the same sizes as other western softwood plywood. Southern pine plywood is also procurable in these sizes.

Hardwood plywood standard sizes are 24, 30, 36, 42, and 48 inches in width and 4, 5, 6, 7, and 8 feet in length. Standard thicknesses are 1/18, 3/16, ¼, 5/16, ⅜, ½, ⅝, ¾, 13/16, 7/8, and 1 inch.

Much hardwood plywood is custom made to special orders

from manufacturers of furniture and similar products, who are concerned primarily with appearance and cut-to-size panels. There is, however, a substantial volume of hardwood plywood manufactured in stock sizes, including 4-foot by 8-foot. Important savings in costs can be realized by adjusting requirements for general-purpose plywood to the sizes normally produced.

Plywood Grades and Standards

The grade of plywood refers to the quality of veneer used for the faces and inner plies. These grades are defined in certain commercial standards that have been accepted by the plywood manufacturers. These are —

CS45   Douglas-fir plywood.
CS35   Hardwood plywood.
CS122   Western softwood plywood.
CS157   Pine plywood (ponderosa pine, sugar pine, and Idaho white pine).
CS259   Southern pine plywood.

The commercial standards for Douglas-fir (CS45) and for western softwoods (CS122), both provide for five grades of veneer: N, A, B, C, and D. Grade N, which is intended for natural finish, is all heartwood free of open defects; a limited number of repairs are permitted. Grade A, suitable for painting, must be free from knots, knotholes, splits, pitch pockets, and other open defects, but glued-in, boat-shaped patches are permitted. Grade B, solid and generally free from open defects, permits sound knots up to 1 inch, circular plugs, and tight splits. Grade C may contain knotholes no larger than 1 inch in least dimension and other open defects of limited size. Grade D permits knotholes no larger than 2-1/2 inches in maximum dimension and other defects of specified limits. Plywood grades are named according to the grade of face and back veneers. For the most part, inner plies of Interior type plywood are of grade D and inner plies of Exterior type are of grade C.

Commercial Standard CS45 also provides for two types of plywood overlaid with resin-impregnated paper. One type (high density) requires that the overlay be no less than 0.009 inch thick, weight no less than 60 pounds per 1,000 square feet, and that no less than 40 percent of the weight of the overlay be a phenol or melamine resin. The surface should be of such a character that further finishing by paint or varnish is not required. The other type (Medium density) requires that the overlay contain no less than 20 percent of phenol or melamine resin, that it be no less than 0.012 inch thick and weigh no less than 65 pounds per 1,000 square feet. The surface should be suitable for painting. The grade of veneer immediately below the high-density overlays may be A or B, as ordered. Veneers immediately below the medium-density overlays are grade B. All inner plies are grade B.

The bulk of the hardwood plywood is produced east of the Mississippi River. It includes many species that vary widely in texture and density. Some, like basswood and cottonwood, are classed as hardwoods but are very soft and light. At the other extreme, birch, beech, and maple are hard and heavy. The factories producing hardwood plywood are more numerous and generally smaller than those producing softwood plywood. The commercial standard for hardwood plywood (CS35) provides for 5 grades. They are designated as custom grade, good grade (1), sound grade (2), utility grade (3), and backing grade (4). The Custom grade provides for special selections as may be agreed upon by buyer and seller. The requirements for Grade 1 were apparently drawn largely with attention to the desires of the furniture industry. The grade often requires a degree of matching for color and limits the small defects that may be objectionable under a clear finish. Grade 2 requires a sound, smooth surface but permits sound knots up to 3/4 inch in average diameter and burls up to 1 inch in average diameter. Grade 3 permits mineral streaks, stain, patches, tight knots without limit, tight burls without limit, knotholes up to 3/4 inch in average diameter, splits or open joints not exceeding 3/16 inch wide and extending less than half the length of the panel, and crossbreaks no greater in length than permissible knotholes. Grade 4 permits knotholes no greater than 2 inches in maximum diameter, no group of knotholes in any 12-inch square exceeding 4 inches in diameter, and splits no wider than 1 inch. For the most part, the grade of the inner plies is grade 2 or grade 3. The grade of the core in lumber-core plywood may be specified by the buyer.

The commercial standard for ponderosa pine, sugar pine, and Idaho white pine plywood (CS157) describes five grades of the face veneers (N-clear, A-sound, B-solid, C-standard, and D-utility). Briefly, the grade N (clear) prohibits defects that would be objectionable under a clear finish. The grades A (sound) and B (solid) should both be paintable, but grade B permits circular plugs and slightly rougher surfaces than grade A. Grade C (standard) and D (utility) are unsanded permitting limited open defects. Plywood is sometimes requisitioned under this commercial standard for such items as cabinets, inside wall covering, cupboard doors, and similar indoor uses.

The commercial standard for southern pine (CS259) describes five grades of face veneers. Grade N is clear and intended for natural finish. Grade A is suitable for painting. Grade B permits minor sanding and patching defects. Grade C permits sanding defects that will not impair the strength and serviceability of the panel. Grade D may be used only in interior type panels.

Plywood Types

Commercial standards and military specifications, with few exceptions, classify plywood by "types" according to the durability of the glues used. The durability of the glue determines the type of service for which the plywood is suitable on the basis of its resistance to water or dampness. Type, then, designates the durability wanted in the glue line, while "grade denates the durability wanted in the glue line, while "grade" defines the appearance or the defects permitted.

Commercial Standards CS45 for Douglas-fir plywood, CS-122 for western softwood plywood and CS157 for pine plywood (ponderosa pine, sugar pine, and Idaho white pine) provide for two types of plywood, called Interior and Exterior. As the name suggests, the Interior type is glued with an adhesive that will stand up well under conditions that are normally associated with the interior of a building but should not be expected to serve satisfactorily when exposed contiuously to the weather or to conditions of prolonged or repeated dampness where the moisture content of the wood exceeds some 18 percent. The glue bond in the Exterior type is very highly resistant to practically all exposures of water, dampness, and heat. In fact, tests thus far have failed to disclose a method of destroying an Exterior glue bond without destroying the wood.

Commercial Standard CS35 for hardwood plywood provides for four types: Technical, Type I, Type II, and Type III. The durability of the glue joints in Technical and Type I plywood is equal to that of the glue joints in Exterior type softwood plywood, in aircraft plywood, or in plywood for boats and ships. The glue bonds of Type II hardwood plywood are more resistant to moisture than those of Type III. Neither can be expected to perform satisfactorily, however, when exposed for long periods to the weather or other severe service.

Some standard grades and typical uses of Douglas-fir and other western softwood plywoods for construction include:

Type, grade	Typical uses
Exterior type:	
Ext. A-A	Outdoors where appearance of both sides is important, such as fences, signs, boats.
Ext. A-C	Where appearance of one side only is important, such as siding, soffits, fences.
Ext. B-C	Utility outdoor building panel.
Ext. C-rep. C.	Base for tile, linoleum, etc., where unusual moisture conditions exist.
Ext. C-C	Unsanded construction panel with waterproof bond.
Ext. B-B	Concrete form grade for maximum reuse.
Interior type:	
Int. A-A	Indoors where both sides are in view — cabinet doors, built-ins, furniture.
Int. A-D	Where high appearance of only one side is important — paneling, built-ins, backing, underlayment.
Int. B-B	Utility panels used where two smooth sides are required.
Int. C-rep. D.	Underlayment grade — base for tile, linoleum, carpeting.
Int. C-D	Unsanded sheathing or structural grade — sheathing, subflooring, barricades.
Int. B-B	Concrete form plywood.

GLUED LAMINATED CONSTRUCTION

Parallel-grain or laminated construction (fig. 43), as distinguished from crossbanded construction, refers to two or more layers of wood glued together with the grain of all layers approximately parallel. The laminations may vary as to species,

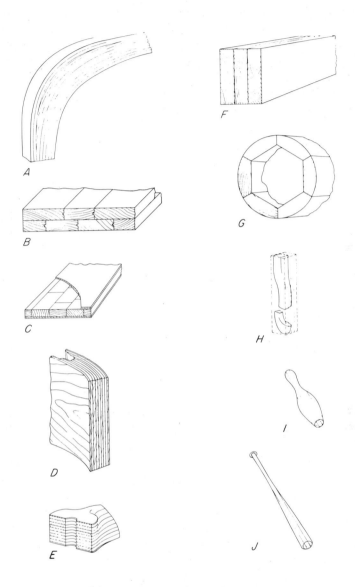

Figure 43. — Types of parallel-grain (laminated) construction: A, Section of arch; B, section of table top; C, section of door stile or rail; D, section of grand piano; E, section of airplane propeller hub; F, section of beam; G, section of a column; H, chair leg; I, bowling pin; J, baseball bat.

number, size, shape, and thickness. Parallel-grain construction finds extensive use as cores for veneered panels and in many unveneered products.

For best results in making laminated glued products it is important to avoid as much as possible the development of internal stresses when the article is exposed to conditions that change its moisture content. Differences in shrinking and swelling are the fundamental causes of internal stresses, and laminations should be of such character that they shrink or swell similar amounts in the same direction.

Gluing together laminations of the same, or different woods that have similar shrinkage characteristics, of all flat-grained or all edge-grained material, and of the same moisture content produces constructions that are the freest from stresses on the glued joints with a minimum of tendency to change shape or the joints to open.

Laminations that have an abnormal tendency to shrink endwise, from such causes as excessive cross grain or the presence of compression wood, should not be included in constructions that must remain flat. Their inclusion may result in serious bowing or cupping of the laminated members.

Strength of Glued Laminated Wood

The properties of parallel-grain constructions are essentially the same as those of solid wood but laminated members, if well constructed, are usually more uniform in strength properties and less apt to change shape with variations in moisture content.

WOOD FOR HANDCARVING

Practically any wood can be used for handcarving. There is, however, a wide range in their workability, as any boy who has ever whittled on a tough knotty pine stick or carved model airplane parts from soft balsa can testify. To list the woods suited to carving into groups based on current demand is impractical since wood sculpture, like ladies' hats, is subject to frequent and marked changes depending upon the whims of the times. Cherry may be the wood for today, whereas walnut may be the favorite tomorrow.

The suitability of woods for carving listed here has been evaluated on a combination of properties. First and foremost are

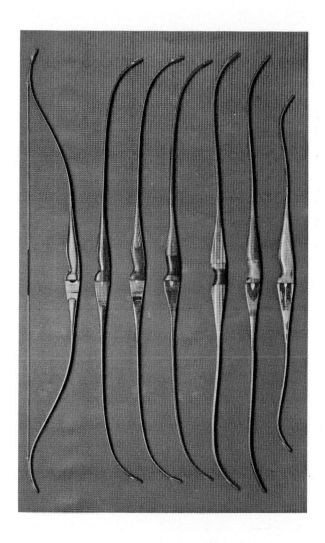

Figure 44. — Archery bows laminated and carved by H. L. Mitchell in home workshop. Chemically stabilized maple veneer used for core lamination.

the smoothness and facility with which it can be cut with sharp handtools, followed by toughness, hardness, freedom from shrinkage and swelling, and lack of tendency to split and warp.

Wood has an advantage over stone, metal, and other materials for sculpturing in that it is easy to handle, readily available, and comes in a wide range of colors and grain patterns. It has long been used as an international medium to symbolize artistry, superb craftsmanship, and candor.

For figures depicting characters that are harsh, rugged, gnarled, homely, or forlorn, the oaks, southern yellow pine, hickory, or maple are used (fig. 45).

For smooth, finished carvings depicting the movement of living creatures, aircraft, or fast boats, fine-grained beautiful woods such as cherry, walnut, ebony, or mahogany, are used.

For sleek animals, feminine grace, or sophisticated young males, walnut, apple, cherry, tupelo, or ebony are favorites (fig. 46).

Most artists chose woods especially suited to the subject. American woods should be used for American bison and rugged frontiersmen in coonskin caps; Asiatic woods should be used for water buffalo and slant-eyed individuals in flat conical hats (fig. 47), and quebracho for bulls of the pampas and gauchos in wide sombreros.

Wood shrinks twice as much in the tangential direction as it does in the radial direction. This frequently results in checking and cracking of the wood if used in the round or in large massive pieces.

Recognition of this fact should be considered in the selection of a wood for carving. No attempt should be made to patch the cracks or splits with the use of fillers, since they are inherent to the use of wood (fig. 48). On the other hand, the use of laminated wood will overcome this deficiency and result in a more satisfactory carving.

Importance of Grain and Figure in Wood

The grain of wood has both a visual and practical effect upon wood as a carving medium. The grain when it follows the contours of a carving enhances the beauty and adds to the strength of the sculpture as wood is stronger along the grain direction than across. Wood also shrinks less along the grain than across the grain.

Suitability for Carving

High	Intermediate	Low
Alder	Baldcypress	Ash
Apple	Blackgum	Aspen
Balsa	Cedar, northern	Douglas-fir
Basswood	white-	Hackberry
Beech	Cedar, westernred	Hemlock, eastern
Birch	Chestnut	Hickory
Boxwood	Cottonwood	Larch, western
Buckeye	Elm, soft	Locust
Butternut	Fir, white	Lignumvitae
Cedar, eastern red	Gumbo-limbo	Pine, southern
Cedar, incense	Hemlock, western	yellow
Cedar, Port-Orford	Jarrah	Tupelo
Cedar, Southern	Karri	
Cherry, black	Laurel	
Chinkapin	Maple, soft	
Cocobolo	Oak, red	
Ebony	Oak, white	
Fir, balsam	Pine, lodgepole	
Holly	Redwood	
Kingwood	Snakewood	
Madrone	Spruce	
Magnolia	Sweetgum	
Mahogany	Sycamore	
Maple, hard	Willow	
Obeche	White afara	
Pear		
Pine, eastern white		
Pine, ponderosa		
Pine, sugar		
Pine, western white		
Rosewood		
Teak		
Walnut		
Yellow-poplar		
Yew		

Figure 45. — White oak effectively used by De Voss to sculpture Op Signor, a folklore character of Belgium.

Figure 46. — Laminated black walnut used by J. C. Killebrew to catch feminine grace in his sculpture, "The Devil is a Lady."

Figure 47. — Local cherry used by Mayalan artist to carve native scene.

A

B

Figure 48. — No attempt should be made to patch cracks and splits, since they are inherent to the use of wood. A. — Knarled and split limb of quebracho effectively used to carve (B) face of natural folklore character.

Figure in wood is the pattern formed by irregular infiltrations of coloring matter; by annual rings and medullary rays; and by cross grain, wavy grain, burls, knots, or other distortion of the normal course of the fibers.

Natural differences in color are comparatively rare in woods, except as the heartwood differs from the sapwood. Circassian walnut, rosewood, some gum, and to a minor extent some black walnut contain darker streaks which give the wood a distinctive figure. In some hardwoods the figure often is made more prominent by the use of dark or, occasionally, light-colored fillers. In conifers unequal absorption produces a like effect.

In many woods in which the color is fairly uniform throughout, some parts look darker than others because of changes in the direction in which the fibers extend, causing light to be reflected differently from different areas. With changes in the angle of vision or of the source of light, the reflection also changes, making the portions of previously dark appear bright, and vice versa. The greater the natural luster of the wood, the more pronounced are such differences in reflection. This is the underlying cause of the beauty of mahogany and many other figured woods; and by virtue of this play of light and shade certain kinds of natural figure can very easily be distinguished from stained or painted imitations.

All woods have some figure, but in many it is so obscure or uninteresting as to receive no consideration (fig. 49). It is because some woods have a distinctly variegated appearance that they are considered superior and are sought by experienced wood sculptors. A uniform color, no matter how rich its tone, does not give so pleasing an effect as the variations in color, lights and shadows, curves and stripes, which form the figure.

No two pieces of wood show the same figure. In this way the natural pattern of wood differs from artificial patterns sometimes painted on wood or metal or incorporated into various fabrics. Thus a wood sculpture for which the wood has been carefully selected and properly carved is an exhibition not only of the mechanical skill of man but also of the beauties of nature which can be revealed to best advantage only by the hand of the artisan (fig. 50).

Once a wood carving has been made, it can be reproduced on a multiple lathe by tracing much as duplicate car keys are

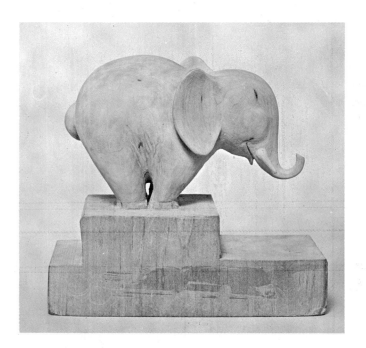

Figure 49. — Basswood, although lacking in grain pattern, is a splendid wood to carve as indicated by Killebrew in this small carving of an elephant.

made, yet each replica will have its own individual and distinctive grain pattern. Like finger prints, no two wood carvings will ever have identical grain patterns.

Wherever possible, carving should be done with the grain since wood is twice as strong with the grain as across the grain. Arms and legs at right angles to the grain are not practical. Even if fashioned with great care they are likely to snap off if dropped, hit, or jolted. Where such projections are necessary, they should be carved separately with the grain and jointed to the body with dowels or other locking devices. Some woods have diagonal or spiral grain and on large sculptures can be fashioned with skill to objects of great beauty. On the other hand, in small carvings, such as toy animals, it is advisable to use straight-grained wood free of knots or other natural defects (fig. 51). No serious difficulty with grain direction is likely to be encountered in carving woods such as apple, cherry, beech, maple, northern white pine, sugar pine, ponderosa pine, sycamore, or mahogany.

Grain or figure are as a rule not so important in relief carving as in sculpture in the round. Relief carving is more closely associated with drawing in wood, the tool marks being used to accentuate the work in contrast to the smoothed quality of the work in the round (fig. 52). An insight into relief carving for the beginner may be had through the close examination of the techniques used in the design of patterns on coins. The play of light and shade on relief carvings is particularly important and the work should be done under lighting conditions similar to that employed where the carving is to be displayed.

Laminated Wood For Carving

Wood bonded with modern adhesives into laminated blocks or other forms is an excellent material for handcarving. Laminated wood has an advantage over solid wood in that the individual boards can be carefully selected and seasoned prior to bonding. Thus, the block to be carved is free of hidden defects and held together with adhesives stronger than the wood itself.

Precatalyzed urea resin glue obtainable in small quantities from local hardware stores is the most satisfactory adhesive for laminating wood blocks for carvings that are to be displayed indoors. This glue should be used at approximately room temperature (70° F.). Use of the glue outdoors in cold winter weather or in cold damp basement workshops is not recommended. This

Figure 50. — Solid walnut containing sapwood and blue stain used effectively by Killebrew to show tarnished beard on carving of hermit.

Figure 51.— Italian carving of toy dog of straight-grained, defect-free wood for maximum strength.

Figure 52. — Southern pine with broad summerwood bands used by Killebrew to show Kentucky colonel.

glue leaves a fine tan glue line that is practically unnoticeable. It stains wood very slightly if at all. It produces joints high in both wet and dry strength. Urea resin is moderately durable even under damp conditions.

Polyvinyl resin is a ready mixed, transparent glue convenient for use in laminating blocks for woodcarving, but it is subject to slippage of joints at either high termperatures or high humidities. The slippage results from internal stresses set up in the different laminations because of change in the moisture content or temperature of the individual boards.

In the carving of laminated wood the adjoining pieces of wood should be matched as to figure, otherwise the play of light upon the grain pattern will distinguish the individual pieces and detract from the overall beauty of the sculpture (fig. 53).

If laminated wood is used for relief carving it is desirable to place the grain pattern so that it is most effective. For example, in the relief carving of the face of Paul Bunyan, the grain of the laminated wood was so selected that it ran diagonally to the base of the panel but parallel to the nose (fig. 54). This arrangement resulted in the play of light that had the effect of making the nose protrude from the panel.

The end grain of laminated wood is especially well suited for the wood engraving of book illustrations (fig. 55).

In handcarving any wood, the cutting edges on the tools must be extremely sharp at all times. This is even more important in carving laminated wood since some glues, when fully cured, have a marked tendency to dull tools.

Sculpturing Hints

The experienced sculptor can glance at a piece of wood and immediately evaluate it for his carving. Frequently the grain and pattern of the wood determine the theme for the carving. For example, the carving of the devil amid flames (fig. 56) was determined by the color and grain distortion in the juniper bolt.

For sculpturing large objects it is frequently advisable to select a wood that will produce smooth surfaces where needed over small areas but can be rough carved for the major portions (fig. 57).

Discarded end of a laminated beam from a church cross used by Killebrew for this religious sculpture (fig. 58). The wood is koa from Hawaii.

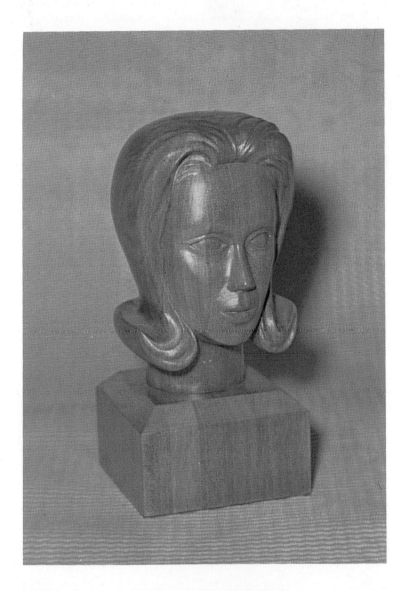

Figure 53.— Laminated mahogany used by Killebrew to carve head of modern girl. Note play of light on the grain of the one lamination that was reversed in the assembly of the laminated block.

Figure 54. — Laminated redwood relief carving of Paul Bunyan's face by Killebrew. Grain of wood selected to make nose appear to protrude from panel.

M 126 273

Figure 55.—Wood engraving made by Killebrew on the end grain of laminated maple. Note razor edge on special cutting tool.

Figure 56. — The red color and grain distortion around knots in the juniper bolt dictated the flame pattern of this carving by Killebrew. The limb portion of two knots was entirely cut out in order to give greater dimension to the piece.

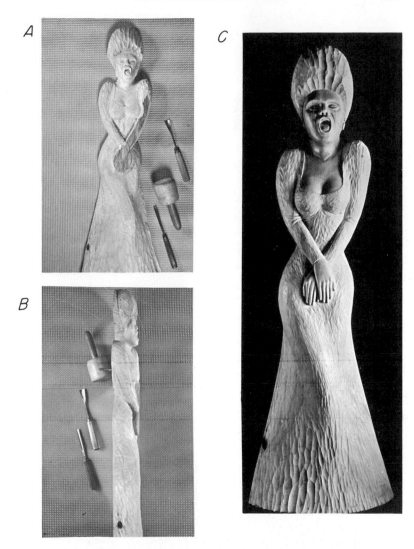

Figure 57. — *Cottonwood slab 45 inches in length used by Killebrew to carve "Torch Singer." Note small area of smooth surface compared with large area of rough surface. A, front view of semifinished stage and sculpturing tools. The bottom of the dress follows contour of slab. Encased knot on left adds interest to design. The sculpturing tools used include (top) 1-inch fishtail gouge, (middle) mallet, (bottom) ½-inch gouge. B, a side view. Note handrail screw (near mallet) used to hold slab during carving. C, finished sculpture.*

Figure 58.—Sculpture by Killebrew from laminated koa. Note the selection of the flat-grained surface to accentuate the forehead and nose.

SOME COMMON FALLACIES ABOUT WOOD

In the course of its more than 50 years of work, the Forest Products Laboratory continues to encounter various false ideas about wood, many of which lead to unnecessary trouble, expense, or dissatisfaction in the use of wood. Some common misconceptions of this kind are the following:

Fallacy 1.—That all wood in the course of time "naturally" decays as a result of age.

This fatalistic concept ignores the true cause of decay and may lead the user to neglect the proper precautions against it. Time or age itself has nothing to do with the decay of wood. The White House, when remodeled in 1949, was found to contain sound timbers that had been in place since 1816. The Fairbanks house, a wood structure in Dedham, Mass., is standing structurally intact after three centuries. Timbers several hundred years old have been recovered from the ruins of Indian pueblos in Arizona and New Mexico. A part of a Roman emperor's houseboat that sank long ago in Lake Nemi was sound enough nearly 2,000 years later to be identified by the Forest Products Laboratory as spruce. A log 1 feet in diameter was found some years ago in a tunnel being dug 150 feet below the bed of the Yakima River in Washington. A piece of it was sent to the Forest Products Laboratory and the wood was identified as an extinct species of sequoia, of an age estimated by geologists at 12 million years. During the progress of thousands or perhaps millions of years wood constantly immersed in water or wet soil gradually undergoes chemical changes (not to be confused with true decay) that result in a loss of some of the original strength.

This millenial process that involves only immersed wood, however, has no practical significance for current structures.

These examples prove that wood does not necessarily decay with age at all. Decay is the result of one thing only, and that is the attack of wood-destroying fungi. In the cases mentioned the wood had been kept free of fungus attack in one of two ways: it had been kept dry, as in weatherproof structures or in a dry climate, or it had been kept thoroughly and permanently saturated. A fungus is a plant. If the wood is too dry for it to grow and spread, decay does not occur. If the wood is throughly saturated, the fungus is "downed out." The range of activity of fungi lies between 20 percent moisture content of the wood and a "soaking wet" condition in which all air is excluded.

Fallacy 2.—That some woods never decay, regardless of exposure and service conditions.

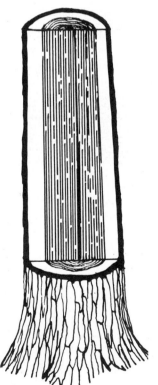

Both this fallacy and the first one are answered by the fact that no woods decay when fully protected from fungi, and that any wood will decay when exposed to fungus attack that is severe enough and continued long enough.

The conditions that bring about decay of wood are, briefly, dampness and mild to warm weather. If you have a house, porch, or shed built over damp, poorly drained ground, with the foundations bricked or boarded in, look out for decay. Sills of untreated wood resting directly on damp ground are sure to rot. Likewise untreated posts and poles set in the ground are exposed to ideal conditions for fungus attack, and their service will usually be terminated by decay near the ground line, no matter what wood is used.

The sapwood of all species is easily and quickly destroyed by decay. (Sapwood is the outer, light-colored part of the tree trunk). But it is a fact that the HEARTWOOD of some species resists decay longer than the heartwood of others. This is the advantage of using for fence posts, and so on, such decay resistant species as cedar, catalpa, chestnut, baldcypress, juniper, black locust, osage-orange or bois d' arc, and redwood. They may last for years. Do not imagine, however, that the underground parts of the post will remain just as you put them in; in a comparatively short time decay will eat away the sapwood, and the business of holding up the fence will be left to a core of the more resistant heartwood. Of course, by treating the wood with a good preservative you change the picture materially. Most of the preservative goes into the sapwood and protects the part that is most vulnerable to decay.

But to suppose that the use of cypress, cedar, or any other special wood will excuse you from all precautions against decay is a bad mistake. Don't expect too much of Nature. In the first place, remember that only the heartwood is the durable part, and then take care of the service conditions as well as you can. A Laboratory man once went to inspect a floor that was falling in. It happened that the subfloor was of genuine cypress, specifically put there to ward off decay, but alas! It was laid directly over damp ground and was covered with tar paper before laying the upper boards. What the owner had was a high-powered fungus pit for his cypress, and the fungus literally ate up the subfloor and spread to other parts of the building at the owner's expense.

Fallacy 3.—That there is such a thing as "dry rot" of wood.

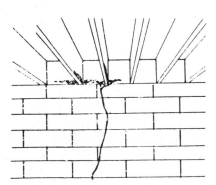

Much has been written or said about "dry rot" in buildings. Any brown, crumbly rot is so called, but the term is a misnomer. No fungus can grow without water. Wood is the food for the wood-destroying fungi, but they cannot use that food unless it contains at least 20 percent of water (based on the weight of the oven-dry wood). However, the fungi that are responsible for some of the decay in buildings are capable of rotting wood that is apparently much drier, for they produce water-conducting strands which carry water from some source, usually in the ground, up into buildings where the wood normally would be dry. Moreover, some wood-destroying fungi can remain dormant in dry wood for months or even years and then revive and continue their destructive work as soon as moisture becomes available.

Call it dry rot if you wish, the fungi that come sneaking into a house carrying their water supply are bad ones, and should have been kept out by proper precautions when the house was built. The Latin name of the most common one in the United States is *Poria incrassata*. It is at home in the South, on the Pacific Coast, and at least as far north as Pennsylvania and Nebraska.

Here is an example: a house was completely wrecked by this destroyer in less than 10 years. Investigation showed that some floor joints were allowed to rest on an old stump that happened to be in just the right place — or the wrong place. Don't give this wrecker a chance to get into your home by leaving planks or timbers connecting the structure with the ground. After *Poria incrassata* gets started it can set up its own connections with the damp ground, an ugly rootlike growth sometimes as big as your finger and thumb.

A good, dry, well-built frame house is in practically no danger from decay if just a few normal precautions are taken. (1) Build on a well-drained site and avoid construction that allows moisture to accumulate in joints or pockets; (2) secure well-seasoned lumber; (3) do not allow the selected material to lie on the ground after it has been delivered on the job; (4) untreated lumber should not be allowed to come in contact with the soil or with foundations or walls which are liable to be damp, and should not be embedded in concrete or masonry without leaving ventilation around the ends of the timbers; (5) wood flooring, unless it has been chemically preserved, should never be laid directly on the soil or on concrete that is in contact with the soil; (6) remember that dry wood will not decay.

Fallacy 4.—That wood used in construction is under all conditions more dangerous than steel in case of fire.

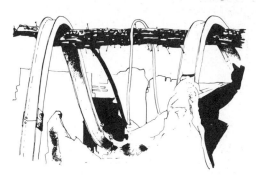

It is true that wood when exposed to fire temperatures will burn and be converted to charcoal, whereas steel does not burn under similar exposure conditions. But wood, when used in heavy timber construction, has a tremendous advantage over unprotected steel. Where thick beams constitute the supporting members of a structure, the outside surfaces, on exposure to severe fire conditions, will become charred, while a substantial core of wood, because of its low heat conductivity, remains at low temperature, uncharred and intact, and retains most of its strength for some time. Steel, under the same fire exposure conditions, because of its good heat conduction, will quickly become heated throughout and lose much of its rigidity and load-bearing capacity and thus permit collapse of a structure sooner than timbers of the same initial strength. For structural purposes, the working strength of unprotected wrought iron and steel as reported in Johnson's Materials of Construction, must be regarded as regularly diminishing while the temperature increases, the rate of diminution being about 4 percent per 100°F. increase in temperature.

It is for this reason that steel members are commonly required to be enclosed in concrete or some other protective material.

Fallacy 5.—That a fence post will give better service if set in the ground "upside down."

A tradition seems to exist in some quarters that setting posts bottom end up (opposite the position of growth) makes them last longer. There is neither evidence nor theoretical basis to support this idea, so far as we are aware. On the contrary we should expect posts so reversed to rot more quickly than if set upright. They would have less material at the ground line for fungus to rot through, and a greater proportion of that material would be sapwood, which is generally an easy prey for fungus. Furthermore, the less wood a post has at the ground line the weaker it is, like a fishing pole grasped at the small end.

Fallacy 6.—That oak, hickory, or other heavy hardwood, has a higher fuel value than pine.

This may be true as between a cord of hickory and a cord of pine, as the cord of hickory weighs more; but pound for pound the pine gives off more heat. Resinous woods in general have a higher heat value per pound than nonresinous. What this means is that for a quick, hot fire you would use pine; but for practical home heating or cooking purposes no general means has yet been devised to "tame down" the burning of resinous woods and make them last like a hickory backlog, for instance.

Fallacy 7.—That the sap "rises" in a tree in the spring and "goes down" in the late fall.

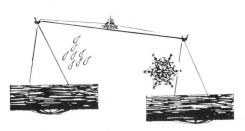

The difference about sap is that it is moving or circulating actively in the spring and summer. It is always "up" and never "down." By actual weighing, logs are heavier in the winter than in spring, showing that they have more sap in the inactive season. If the sap were "down," no tree could freeze in winter as they often do, with a loud "crack."

Fallacy 8.—That trees exposed to storms and rough weather all their lives form stronger and better wood than sheltered trees.

This idea is mere poetic license, as it never affects the selection of wood in manufacture and actual use. Trees exposed to extra severe conditions are apt to be deformed, gnarly, twisted, stunted, and fit mostly for firewood. Trees grown under normal forest conditions make the best lumber because they are straight and regular in grain. Piece for piece, their wood is as strong if not stronger than that grown under the wildest conditions of exposure.

Fallacy 9.—That wood of a given species grown in one State or region is superior to that grown in another State or region.

Examples are "Michigan maple" or "Vermont maple," northern vs. southern ash, etc.

Tests of more than 600,000 specimens at the Forest Products Laboratory prove that a tree's location inside or outside certain imaginary geographical lines has nothing at all to do with the strength of its wood. If the tree or species in question is growing within its proper range of climate, it is not affected by its north, south, east, or west location within that range. The immediate influences of its site, such as moisture, drainage, fertility, and exposure have the controlling effect. Properties of the wood in any one State or region will show a wider variation than any general geographic difference. The test of wood quality lies within the piece or the shipment itself, and not in where it came from.

Fallacy 10.—That limbs rise higher from the ground as the tree grows older.

This phenomenon would obviously require the stretching of the interior wood where the limb is attached, and trees simply do not grow that way. A new layer of wood is put on every year over the tree as it stands, limbs and all. What goes on this year stays put. If there is a limb 10 feet from the ground now, that is where it will be next year, unless it breaks off or is cut off. Increase of thickness of limbs may diminish the distance between limbs or, in the case of the lowest limb of the clear bole or log length below it. Nevertheless the center or pith of each limb remains at its original elevation above the ground.

Fallacy 11.—That an expert can tell the age of a piece of wood by looking at it.

This question sometimes comes up in the case of a violin purporting to be a "genuine Stradivarius," according to a Latin label stuck on the inside. This label, put into thousands of cheap new violins, means nothing to the trade except that the instrument is shaped like a Strad; but to the owner the discovery of the secret Latin inscription is often wildly exciting. Hence, an urgent call to the wood expert to inspect the wood and see "how old it is."

Except for the "aging" of wood in color, which may be purely artificial, the expert can determine the age of wood only by counting the rings in the stump when the tree is cut or by highly technical carbon dating. Looking at a stray piece of wood only shows a certain number of rings or growth layers, telling how many years the piece took to grow; the growth may have occurred since 1900 or away back in the Middle Ages, so far as anybody can tell from a single piece. (The research of Professor Douglass on timbers from the old pueblos is a different story which we can hardly go into here.)

Fallacy 12.—That some woods "breed" bedbugs and cockroaches; meaning, perhaps that some woods favor the development of such vermin within their cracks and crannies.

The insects in question appear supremely indifferent to the kind of wood of which a house is built; their interest lies in other directions. To blame poor housekeeping on one or another species of wood of which the house is built is grossly unfair to Mother Nature.

Fallacy 13.—That lumber on the market today is not what it used to be in the "good old days."

Popular opinion to the contrary notwithstanding, timber cut today is as good as Paul Bunyan ever laid ax to. Lumber is now machined better, graded better, and seasoned better than formerly. In addition, a wider selection of species and items is available. It is true that strong competition between dealers and between materials in some localities has resulted in bringing on the market lumber that is not what it should be with respect to size, grade, and seasoning. However, this does not mean that good lumber is not available at economical prices. It does mean that discrimination is necessary in buying lumber as well as in buying other materials — undoubtedly more necessary today than it was in the past.

Fallacy 14.—That wood exposed to very low temperatures is "brittle as glass" and has little strength.

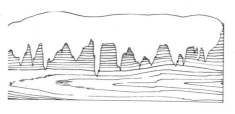

Some people have had the idea that when wood is frozen or exposed to very low temperatures, as in arctic regions, it is seriously damaged and loses most of its strength. There have been reports that a piece of wood dropped on the frozen ground is likely to shatter into small pieces, much as though it were made of glass. Careful investigation has failed to produce any real evidence of such occurrences. Occasionally, a piece of wood of the commonly used species may have natural characteristics, such as knots or slope of grain, that are very severe and damaging to the strength, or the piece may have such low density that it could readily break when dropped or mishandled, even at normal temperatures.

The fact is that tests on wood at temperatures as low as 300° below zero (F.) show that the strength properties of dry wood, including shock resistance, increase as the temperature is reduced. In the case of wood that is saturated with water, the expansion of the water upon freezing may sometimes cause the wood to crack open (see Fallacy 7), but evidence indicates that wet wood also increases in strength when the temperature is reduced.

It is possible that fastenings, such as nails and screws, may tend to loosen somewhat in wood that is repeatedly frozen and thawed, much as they do in wood that is repeatedly wetted and dried. If this does occur, however, it would be a slow process.

Fallacy 15.—That gluing of wood involves a mechanical attachment in which the liquid adhesive flows or is forced into the pores or cavities in the wood where it hardens and becomes anchored somewhat below the surface.

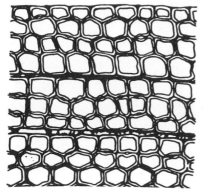

Although some mechanical interlocking may occur in some porous woods and may actually raise the bond strength, the actual adhesion is probably due to chemical or physical forces, similar to those that hold the atoms and molecules of the wood elements themselves together. These forces are often referred to as primary and secondary valence forces. This type of adhesion is often called "specific adhesion."

GLOSSARY

Air-dried. *(See Seasoning.)*

Annual growth ring. (See Ring, annual growth.)

Bastard sawn. Hardwood lumber in which the annual rings make angles of 30 to 60° with the surface of the piece.

Bird's-eye. A small central spot with the wood fibers arranged around it in the form of an ellipse so as to give the appearance of an eye.

Blemish. Anything, not necessarily a defect, marring the appearance of wood.

Boards. (See Lumber.)

Bow. That distortion of a board in which the face is convex or concave longitudinally.

Brash. A condition of wood characterized by low resistance to shock and by an abrupt failure across the grain without splintering.

Broad-leaved trees. (See Hardwoods.)

Burl. A large wartlike excrescence on a tree trunk. It contains the dark piths of a large number of buds which rarely develop. The formation of a burl apparently results from an injury to the tree.

Cambium. The layer of tissue just beneath the bark from which the new wood and bark cells of each year's growth develop.

Cell. A general term for the minute units of wood structure. It includes fibers, vessel segments, and other elements of diverse structure and functions.

Check. A lengthwise separation of the wood, the greater part of which occurs across the rings of annual growth.

Close-grained wood. (See Grain.)

Coarse-grained wood. (See Grain.)

Collapse. The flattening of single cells or rows of cells in heartwood during the drying or pressure treatment of wood, characterized externally by a caved-in or corrugated appearance.

Compression wood. Abnormal wood that often forms on the lower side of branches and of leaning trunks of softwood trees. Compression wood is identified by its relatively wide annual rings, usually eccentric, and its relatively large amount of summerwood, usually more than 50 per cent of the width of the annual rings in which it occurs. Compression wood shrinks excessively lengthwise as compared with normal wood.

Conifer. (See Softwoods.)

Core. The center ply or plies of plywood or other crossbanded products.

Crook. That distortion of a board in which the edge is convex or concave longitudinally.

Crossband. To place the grain of layers of wood at right angles in order to minimize shrinking and swelling and consequent warping; also the layer of veneer at right angles to the face plies.

Cross break. A separation of the wood cells across the grain. Such breaks may be due to internal strains resulting from unequal longitudinal shrinkage or to external forces.

Cross grain. (See Grain.)

Cup. The distortion of a board in which the face is convex or concave transversely.

Decay. Disintegration of wood substance through the action of wood-destroying fungi.

Incipient decay. The early stage of decay in which the disintegration has not proceeded far enough to soften or otherwise impair the hardness of the wood perceptibly.

Typical or advanced decay. The stage of decay in which the disintegration is readily recognized because the wood has become punky, soft and spongy, stringy, pitted, or crumbly.

Deciduous trees. Trees the leaves of which fall at the end of the growing period.

Defect. Any irregularity occurring in or on wood that may lower its strength.

Defoliation. To strip or become stripped of leaves.

Density. The mass of a body per unit volume. When expressed in the metric system, it is numerically equal to the specific gravity of the same substance.

Diagonal grain. (See Grain.)

Diffuse-porous woods. Hardwoods in which the pores are practically uniform in size throughout each annual ring, or decrease slightly toward the outer border of the ring.

Dimension. (See Lumber.)

Dimension stock. Squares or flat stock usually in pieces under the minimum sizes admitted in standard lumber grades, rough or dressed, green or dry, cut to the approximate dimensions required for the various products of woodworking factories.

Dote. "Dote", "doze", and "rot" are synonymous with "decay", and are any form of decay which may be evident as either a discoloration or a softening of the wood.

Durability. A general term for permanence or lastingness. Frequently used to refer to the degree of resistance of a species or of an individual piece of wood to attack by wood-destroying fungi under conditions that favor such attack. In this connection the term "resistance to decay" is more specific.

Edge grain. (See Grain.)

Encased knot. (See Knot.)

Extractives. Substances in wood, not an integral part of the cellular structure, that can be dissolved out with hot or cold water, ether, benzene, or other relatively inert solvents.

Equilibrium moisture content. The moisture content at which wood neither gains nor loses moisture when surrounded by air at a given relative humidity and temperature.

Factory and shop lumber. (See Lumber.)

Fiber. A wood fiber is a comparatively long (one-twenty-fifth or less to one-third inch), narrow, tapering cell closed at both ends.

Fiber-saturation point. The stage in the drying or in the wetting of wood at which the cell walls are saturated and the cell cavities are free from water.

Figure. The pattern produced in a wood surface by irregular coloration and by annual growth rings, rays, knots, and such deviations from regular grain as interlocked and wavy grain.

Flakes. (See Rays, wood.)

Flat grain. (See Grain.)

Flitch. A thick piece of lumber with wane (bark) on one or more edges.

Fungi. Low forms of plant life that attack wood causing molds, stains, or decay.

Grade. The designation of the quality of a manufactured piece of wood.

Grain. The direction, size, arrangement, appearance, or quality of the fibers in wood.

Closed-grained wood. Wood with narrow and inconspicuous annual rings. The term is sometimes used to designate wood having small and closely spaced pores, but in this sense the term "fine textured" is more often used.

Coarse-grained wood. Wood with wide and conspicuous annual rings; that is, rings in which there is considerable difference between springwood and summerwood. The term is sometimes used to designate wood with large pores, such as oak, ash, chestnut, and walnut, but in this sense the term "coarse textured" is more often used.

Cross grain. Grain not parallel with the axis of a piece. It may be either diagonal or spiral grain or a combination of the tree.

Diagonal grain. Annual rings at an angle with the axis of a piece as a result of sawing at an angle with the bark of the tree.

Edge grain. Edge-grain lumber has been sawed parallel with the pith of the log and approximately at right angles to the growth rings; that is, the rings form an angle of 45° or more with the surface of the piece.

Flat grain. Flat-grain lumber has been sawed parallel with the pith of the log and approximately tangent to the growth rings; that is, the rings form an angle of less than 45° with the surface of the piece.

Interlocked-grained wood. Wood in which the fibers are inclined in one direction in a number of rings of annual growth, then gradually reverse and are inclined in an opposite direction in succeeding growth rings, then reverse again.

Open-grained wood. Common classification of painters for woods with large pores, such as oak, ash, chestnut, and walnut. Also known as "coarse textured."

Plain-sawed. Another term for edge grain.

Quarter-sawed. Another term for edge grain.

Spiral grain. A type of growth in which the fibers take a spiral course about the bole of a tree instead of the normal vertical course. The spiral may extend right-handed or left-handed around the tree trunk.

Vertical grain. Another term for edge grain.

Wavy-grained wood. Wood in which the fibers collectively take the form of waves or undulations.

Green. Unseasoned, wet.

Growth ring. (See Ring, annual growth.)

Hardwoods. The botanical group of trees that are broadleaved. The term has no reference to the actual hardness of the wood. Angiosperms is the botanical name for hardwoods.

Heart, Heartwood. The wood, extending from the pith to the sapwood, the cells of which no longer participate in the life processes of the tree. Heartwood may be infiltrated with gums, resins, and other materials which usually make it darker and more decay-resistant than sapwood.

Honeycomb. Checks, often not visible at the surface, that occur in the interior of a piece, usually along the wood rays.

Interlocked-grained wood. (See Grain.)

Kiln. A heated chamber for drying lumber.

Kiln dried. (See Seasoning.)

Knot. That portion of a branch or limb that has become incorporated in the body of a tree.

Decayed knot. A knot which, due to advanced decay, is not so hard as the surrounding wood.

Encased knot. A knot whose rings of annual growth are not intergrown with those of the surrounding wood.

Intergrown knot. A knot whose rings of annual growth are completely intergrown with those of the surrounding wood.

Round knot. A knot whose sawed section is oval or circular.

Sound knot. A knot which is solid across its face and which is as hard as the surrounding wood.

Spike knot. A branch or limb which in the process of lumber manufacture has been sawed in a lengthwise direction.

Laminated wood. A piece of wood built up of plies or laminations that have been joined either with glue or with mechanical fastenings. The term is most frequently applied where the plies are too thick to be classified as veneer and when the grain of all plies is parallel.

Lumber. The product of the saw and planing mill not further manufactured than by sawing, resawing, and passing lengthwise through a standard planing machine, crosscut to length and matched.

> *Factory and shop lumber.* Lumber intended to be cut up for use in further manufacture. It is graded on the basis of the percentage of the area which will produce a limited number of cuttings of a specified, or a given minimum, size and quality.

> *Yard lumber.* Lumber that is less than 5 inches in thickness and is intended for general building purposes.

>> *Boards.* Yard lumber less than 2 inches thick, 8 inches or more in width.

>> *Dimension.* All yard lumber except boards, strips, and timbers; that is, yard lumber 2 inches and less than 5 inches thick, and of any width.

>> *Strips.* Yard lumber less than 2 inches thick and less than 8 inches wide.

Millwork. Generally all building materials made of finished wood and manufactured in millwork plants and planing mills are included under the term "millwork". It includes such items as inside and outside doors, window and door frames, blinds, porch work, mantels, panel work, stairways, moldings, and interior trim. It does not include flooring, ceiling, or siding.

Moisture content of wood. Weight of the water contained in the wood usually expressed in percentage of the weight of the oven-dry wood.

Moisture gradient. A condition of graduated moisture content between the successive layers of a material, such as wood, due to the losing or absorbing of moisture. During seasoning the gradations are between the moisture content of the relatively dry surface layers and the wet layers at the center of the piece.

Open-grained wood. (See Grain.)

Peck. Pockets or areas of disintegrated wood caused by advanced stages of localized decay in the living tree. It is usually associated with cypress and incense cedar. There is no further development of peck once the lumber is seasoned.

Pitch pocket. An opening extending parallel to the annual rings of growth usually containing, or which has contained, pitch, either solid or liquid.

Pith. The small soft core occurring in the structural center of a log.

Plain-sawed. (See Grain.)

Planing mill products. Products worked to pattern, such as flooring, ceiling, and siding.

Plywood. A piece of wood made of three or more layers of veneer joined with glue and usually laid with the grain of adjoining plies at right angles. Almost always an odd number of plies is used to secure balanced construction.

Pocket rot. Advanced decay which appears in the form of a hole, pocket, or area of soft rot usually surrounded by apparently sound wood.

Pore. (See Vessel.)

Preservative. Any substance that, for a reasonable length of time, will prevent the action of wood-destroying fungi, borers of various kinds, and similar destructive life when the wood has been properly coated or impregnated with it.

Quarter-sawed. (See Grain.)

Radial. Coincident with a radius from the axis of the tree or log to the circumference.

Rate of growth. The rate at which a tree has laid on wood, measured radially in the trunk or in lumber cut from the trunk. The unit of measure in use is the number of annual growth rings per inch.

Rays, wood. Strips of cells extending radially within a tree and varying in height from a few cells in some species to 4 inches or more in oak. The rays serve primarily to store food and transport it horizontally in the tree.

Refractory woods. Woods which are especially resistant to ordinary treatment.

Ring, annual growth. The growth layer put on in a single growth year.

Ring-porous woods. A group of hardwoods in which the pores are comparatively large at the beginning of each annual ring and decrease in size more or less abruptly toward the outer portion of the ring, thus forming a distinct inner zone of pores known as the springwood and the outer zone with smaller pores known as the summerwood.

Rot. (See Decay.)

Rotary-cut veneer. (See Veneer.)

Sap. All the fluids in a tree, special secretions and excretions, such as gum, excepted.

Sapwood. The layers of wood next to the bark, usually lighter in color than the heartwood, one-half inch to 3 or more inches wide that are actively involved in the life processes of the tree. Under most conditions sapwood is more susceptible to decay than heartwood; as a rule, it is more permeable to liquids than heartwood. Sapwood is not essentially weaker or stronger than heartwood of the same species.

Sawed veneer. (See Veneer.)

Seasoning. Removing moisture from green wood in order to improve its serviceability.

Air-dried or air seasoned. Dried by exposure to the air, usually in a yard, without artificial heat.

Kiln dried. Dried in a kiln with the use of artificial heat.

Second growth. Timber that has grown after the removal by any means of all or a large portion of the previous stand.

Shake. A separation along the grain, the greater part of which occurs between the rings of annual growth.

Shop lumber. (See Lumber.)

Sliced veneer. (See Veneer.)

Softwoods. The botanical group of trees that have needle or scalelike leaves and are evergreen for the most part, cypress, larch, and tamarack being exceptions. The term has no reference to the actual hardness of the wood. Softwoods are often referred to as conifers, and botanically they are called gymnosperms.

Specific gravity. The ratio of the weight of a body to the weight of an equal volume of water at some standard temperature.

Spiral grain. (See Grain.)

Split. A lengthwise separation of the wood, due to the tearing apart of the wood cells.

Springwood. The portion of the annual growth ring that is formed during the early part of the season's growth. It is usually less dense and weaker mechanically than summerwood.

Stain, blue. A bluish or grayish discoloration of the sapwood caused by the growth of certain moldlike fungi on the surface and in the interior of the piece; made possible by the same conditions that favor the growth of other fungi.

Stain, chemical brown. A chemical discoloration of wood, which sometimes occurs during the air drying or the kiln drying of several species, apparently caused by the oxidation of extractives.

Strength. The term in its broader sense embraces collectively all the properties of wood which enable it to resist different forces or loads. In its more restricted sense, strength may apply to any one of the mechanical properties, in which event the name of the property under consideration should be stated, thus strength in compression parallel to the grain, strength in bending, hardness, etc.

Structural timber. Pieces of wood of relatively large size in which strength is the controlling element in their selection and use. Trestle timbers (stringers, caps, posts, sills, bracing, bridge ties, guard rails); car timbers (car framing, including upper framing, car sills); framing for buildings (posts, sills, girders, framing joists); ship timbers (ship timbers, ship decking); and crossarms for poles are examples of structural timbers.

Summerwood. The portion of the annual growth ring that is formed during the latter part of the yearly growth period. It is usually more dense and stronger mechanically than springwood.

Tangential. Strictly, coincident with a tangent at the circumference of a tree or log, or parallel to such a tangent. In practice, however, it often means roughly coincident with a growth ring.

Texture. A term often used interchangeably with grain. In this factbook it refers to the finer structure of the wood (see Grain) rather than to the annual rings.

Timber, standing. Timber still on the stump.

Tracheid. The elongated cells that constitute the greater part of the structure of the softwoods (frequently referred to as fibers). Also a portion of some hardwoods.

Twist. A distortion caused by the turning or winding of the edges of a board so that the four corners of any face are no longer in the same plane.

Veneer. Thin sheets of wood.

    Rotary-cut veneer. Veneer cut in a continuous strip by rotating a log against the edge of a knife in a lathe.

    Sawed veneer. Veneer produced by sawing.

    Sliced veneer. Veneer that is sliced off by moving a log, bolt, or flitch against a large knife.

Vertical grain. (See Grain.)

Vessels. Wood cells of comparatively large diameter which have open ends and are set one above the other forming continuous tubes. The openings of the vessels on the surface of a piece of wood are usually referred to as pores.

Virgin growth. The original growth of mature trees.

Wane. Bark, or lack of wood or bark, from any cause, on edge or corner of a piece.

Warp. Any variation from a true or plane surface. Warp includes bow, crook, cup, and twist, or any combination thereof.

Wavy-grained wood. (See Grain.)

Weathering. The mechanical or chemical disintegration and discoloration of the surface of wood that is caused by exposure to light, the action of dust and sand carried by winds, and the alternate shrinking and swelling of the surface fibers that come with the continual variation in moisture content brought by changes in the weather. Weathering does not include decay.

Wood preservative. (See Preservative.)

Workability. The degree of ease and smoothness of cut obtainable with hand or machine tools.

INDEX